Also by Shoshana Kobrin

The Satisfied Soul Daily GuideBook:
Your Path to Fulfillment

The Satisfied Soul:
Transforming Your Food and Weight Worries

Love, Anger, Power – and Food!
A GuideBook for Women

DO NO HARM
TRANSFORMING
ADDICTIONS

Shoshana Kobrin, MA, MFT

Kobrin Kreations

WALNUT CREEK, CALIFORNIA

Do No Harm/Shoshana Kobrin — 1st ed.
ISBN-13: 978-09908854805
ISBN-10: 0990885402

Library of Congress Number: 2014915419

The stories in the text bear no reference to any one person.
Confidentiality has been strictly observed.
This book is not a substitute for professional help.

Kobrin Kreations
http://www.shoshanakobrin.net/
shoshanakobrin@gmail.com

Printed in the United States of America

For my grandchildren:

Lily, Tula, David, Shaina, and Ethan

Be the change you wish to see in the world.
—Gandhi

Acknowledgments

Loc Huynh, web wizard with Buddha-like patience, who formatted the covers

Connie Wisean, psychic healer and teacher

Hollie Holmes-Meredith, Reiki instructor

Kathleen Epperson for her help, support, and tuition with my editing and proofreading

Ruth Schwartz who formatted this book

The addiction specialists who so graciously gave me their time and expertise for interviews, adding another dimension to my knowledge of addictions

Roberta Meyer, also an interviewee, who is in hospice with cancer—may she go gently into the light

My friends and neighbors: Don Basset and his fox terrier, Buddy, Ruth Schauer and her chihuahua, Robin, and Angie Logsdon, walking partner

Albione Becnel, Judy Schavrien, and Gretchen Smith for their contributions to this book

All those who shared their stories of addiction and recovery

And especially:

My spiritual guides who return me to the path however much I stray

Live as if you were to die tomorrow,
learn as if you were to live forever.
— Gandhi

Table of Contents

OVERTURE

HARMFUL HABITS

DO YOU CORKSCREW into a harmful habit when stressed? Are you trapped into a never-ending cycle of attempt and failure? Do you spend far beyond your budget? Do you try in vain to give up pot, six packs of Coors each Saturday night, Danish pastries for breakfast, Internet pornography sites, gambling, or cigarette smoking? After each reprieve, does the addictive process start up all over again? Do you blame yourself? Have you lost hope that things can ever change?

I write this book as an insider. I have a bone-deep familiarity with the struggle of addiction and its strenuous healing. This book is based on personal experience of a food addiction. For 23 years I was a victim to bulimia. My first thought on waking each morning was whether I should abstain or indulge. I disliked myself, loathed every inch of my body. I've spent more years – and money – on psychotherapy than you would care to know! Psychotherapy was valuable, but not enough to resolve the addiction. Buddhist Vipassana meditation, mindfulness, journaling, chakra clearing, Reiki, and self-help exercises led to recovery and harmony with my life.

With my history it was natural to enter the field of counseling. As a psychotherapist for 27 years, I have counseled clients and trained therapists and interns. I've conducted workshops, courses, and retreats on the addictive process and its recovery. *Do No Harm* covers all the major addictions.

In addition to a significant amount of research, I interviewed professionals with a wide range of approaches to addictions. Each professional has considerable expertise with a particular addiction and methodology.

Today many of us struggle with addictive substances and behaviors: drugs, alcohol, food, gambling, sex, overspending, nicotine, caffeine, or Internet addiction. With the proliferation of mobile phones, misusing texting, computer surfing, and Internet browsing has reached epidemic proportions.

Harmful habits that take over our lives prevent us from fully living. The way out is to step back, take a look at ourselves and how we interact with life. Your reading this means you're ready to make changes. Or perhaps an important person in your life – friend, partner, child, parent – is struggling with a harmful habit. And you've reached the point where you're compelled to step in. This book is also geared for those in the healing professions.

As you read on, you'll see many factors which contributed to your addiction. People with addictions are belittled and discriminated against. It's vital that you don't blame yourself. Your addiction was a way to survive arduous circumstances. It's time to learn self-compassion and self-care.

Perhaps now you've decided that there's more to life than a double scotch or perusing catalogs for the latest toy. Do you long for something more satisfying and fulfilling? Do you feel the urge to discover unknown aspects of yourself – hidden talents, gifts, and capabilities? Give yourself permission to develop and gratify those parts of yourself. This book will help you to step into rich and prosperous living.

What is a Habit?

How are habits started? Many of them are routine mindless behaviors necessary to keep the wheels of our day running smoothly. We make the bed when we rise in the morning, brush teeth, and prepare our breakfast eggs. Settled practices are indeed hard to give up. Judy, one of my clients, repeatedly took U.S. Route 34 W instead of her usual Highway 56 N after moving from one part of town to another.

What Is an Addiction?

A substance-based addiction is a compulsive need for a habit-forming substance such as drugs, alcohol, sugar, nicotine, or caffeine. Process-based or behavioral addictions are gambling, excessive Internet use, or a food, sex, or spending compulsion. Even when we know the addiction is physically, psychologically, and socially harmful, we can't control it.

Harmful Habits

Perhaps you, like many of us, feel that "addiction" or "addict" are derogatory terms. An "addict" is stereotyped as unwashed, scruffy, homeless, and hitting the skids. So I do not use this term. Many of the sources I quote freely use "addiction." I prefer "harmful habit." However, since "addiction" is a well-known, broad-based, catch-all and a handy, shortcut that allows writing to flow, I use both words interchangeably. "Addictive" refers to a harmful substance or behavior.

When is a habit harmful? Suppose you enjoy a cup of carefully selected mocha java at the Corner Coffee Hut with your buddies. This activity enhances your life so I would not term it a harmful habit. However, if you depend on cup after cup to keep you going during the day and you have insomnia, headaches, nausea, anxiety, and irritability because of it, then you have a harmful habit. Playing computer games becomes harmful when it replaces most of the time spent with your family and friends. When it damages your body, work, relationships, and parenting ability. The key words here are "excessive," and "compulsive." If you cannot start the day without your glass of Chardonnay, this habit will probably escalate. It could have dangerous repercussions. The word "dependence" accurately describes a harmful habit: "He is dependent on alcohol." You feel you cannot live without your habit. You have no choice. You're attempting to feel satisfied by the harmful behavior. You are relieving withdrawal rather than experiencing the full range of a loving and rewarding life.

> Marjorie is no derelict off the streets. She is the mother of three school-age children. Her husband works two jobs and takes the kids on weekends because she is too stoned to care for them or to work. She started on drugs for pain relief when she fell and broke her back in three places. Over the years, with a shoulder pulled out of joint by a dog too big for her to handle and carpal tunnel from her computer job, she gradually became accustomed to Oxycodone's buzz.
>
> At first, the withdrawal from only three or four pills a day was annoying, but mild. Xanax eased the pain of that withdrawal. Then she stocked up on prescription drugs to avoid the hassle of running out on a weekend when no doctor was available. She'd plead with her primary care physician, "I really need my pain medication. Please, please give me another prescription."

How to Use This Book

My approach is holistic. It involves your whole self and your whole life. As you understand the deeper layers of your struggle, as you become more accepting of yourself and your life, your preoccupation with the addiction will lose its hold.

Do No Harm is designed to give you a quick start. It's divided into three parts. The first part, *Overture*, outlines and defines the features of an addiction, gives statistics on the various types of addictions, and surveys the most important points. It includes an overview of the book's basic ideas and concepts.

In the second part, *Causes*, we explore the factors that brought you to this point. Appreciating how and why your addiction developed is vital for releasing guilt and self-blame. A crucial step toward recovery is no longer feeling there's something permanently wrong with you. There are clear-cut reasons that brought you to this point. Knowing them will free you from the false belief that you're doomed to struggle with your harmful habit forever and ever.

The chapter on *American Dreaming* is how our culture promotes addictions. You'll see the effect of discrimination on people suffering with addictions. Having struggled for years with my food addiction, I make no judgments on those with other harmful habits.

The third part, *Solutions*, gives you new concepts and practical tools to heal the addiction.

The book contains significant amounts of statistics and research. Please feel free to glide over these if you're more interested in the practical side of healing addictions.

In the text are two types of boxes. One contains points made by a specialist whom I've interviewed. The other type contains vignettes or case histories – short stories illustrating the text. Although these stories in the boxes and in the text are based on real people and their experiences, they are products of my imagination. They bear no reference to any one person.

Confidentiality has been strictly observed. I trust these stories will resonate with you and aid you in your healing journey.

Do No Harm is not a substitute for professional treatment. A list of resources is at the end of this book.

THE DARK SPIRAL AND THE SATISFIED SOUL

The Dark Spiral

ADDICTIONS ARE AN UNCONSCIOUS effort to survive a lack of meaning in ourselves and in life. We believe we're undeserving and insignificant. Our lives feel empty, futile and pointless. In *Imaginary Crimes* Lewis and Engel describe this as believing we are "Basically Bad," all the way down to the marrow of our bones. Do you operate from this false and deeply unconscious belief about yourself? Are you hooked into the "scarcity principle" – that there will never be sufficient love, joy or happiness for you?

Are you convinced that no matter how hard you try, you'll never succeed? This belief is confirmed when attempts to quit an addiction fail. There you are, spiraling down again, sad, mad, and frustrated with yourself.

Depriving yourself of emotional satisfaction is characteristic of harmful habits. I call this belief system "the Dark Spiral." When we're lost in this spiral's inner emptiness, our lives feel mundane and useless. We question whether there's a greater purpose in living. Do important areas in your life deplete rather than nourish you? When you're reaching for a cigarette, a second Bloody Mary, a sugary soda, or sifting through Internet porn sites, are you attempting to fill that emptiness? Willpower is not enough to fix this.

> Mary Lou, recently a widow, is 67 years old. She struggles with depression and ongoing symptoms of post-menopause. Food, especially chocolate, is a major source of comfort for her. This results in a substantial weight gain. She often wonders if there's more to life than climbing out of bed in the morning, making coffee, browsing the newspaper, then sitting in front of the TV. She asks, "What is my life all about? I'm born, I live, I die – is that all? No excitement, no passion, nothing about me or how I live is of any consequence."

If you struggle with the Dark Spiral of addictions, you probably have difficulty in forming positive connections with your emotions, body, family, relationships, community, vocation, and living situation.

Connecting with your Inner Core Self – your authentic self – and what gives meaning to your life is also difficult. Let's look at these important aspects of life in more detail.

Emotions

Do you turn to heroin, gamble, or immerse yourself in an Internet game to numb emotions that are so hard to bear? A harmful habit pushes down the emotional wounds, both present and past, of rejection, anger, misunderstanding, or abuse.

Body

Do you find it easy to criticize your body? Hard to appreciate it? Are you unaware of body signals? Do you ignore hunger, tension, and fatigue? Did you learn as a child to disconnect from bodily sensations? Is it simpler to stay with what works, even though it doesn't?

Family, Relationships, and Community

You may catch yourself thinking: "I'll never get the love I want. I'm just not loveable. Wherever I am, I never belong." Whether we're with our family, friends, or attending a class, those of us with addictions constantly feel like outcasts. We never quite fit in.

Your family of origin formed the groundwork of who you are. Did you feel loved and accepted? If your parents didn't raise you, who did and why? What memories stand out? Are they good or bad? Was your extended family important to you? What is your relationship with your family now?

Is your harmful habit your closest friend? Better, more consistent and trustworthy than any relationship? Do you have a pattern of avoiding closeness or conflict?

All relationships have their conflicts. Addictions make it easy to deny and ignore problems.

Vocation

Whether you're part of the work force, a student, or retiree, how you spend your day is an indication of either life-satisfaction or the inner emptiness of addiction. The word "vocation" comes from the Latin "vocātiō," a call or summons. Too many of us sacrifice job satisfaction for money. Our daily toil feels like a grind instead of a calling. Is this the vocation you've always longed for? What do you like and dislike about it?

Living Situation

Missing a sense of place, feeling unconnected to where we live, is a facet of the Dark Spiral. Do you stay in a place because it's familiar or the job is good? While these are important considerations, they can keep us in our familiar addictive patterns.

Your Inner Core Self

Those of us struggling with harmful habits are often taught to be "nice," to conceal the "me within me." We present a false self. We chair yet another committee or offer to be the designated driver so our pals can have a good time at the bar. Pleasing others at the expense of our own needs triggers doubts about who we really are. Do you wonder, "Am I valued for who I am or only for what I do for others?"

What roles do you play in life? How do you feel about yourself in each? Do they reflect the person you are, the person you would like to be?

"Who am I?" Abhilasha asks in her journal. "Just the Hand writing the check for electricity and gas; the Wage Earner, smile-smile at my colleagues day after day; the Wife, fresh sheets on the double bed; the Hostess, dinner chat, small talk. Is that all I am?" When trying on designer dresses at Fifth Avenue Mall, Abhilasha spins one way then another before the mirror. This gives her a sense of herself she is unable to access in any other way. That's how her full-scale spending addiction started.

The Satisfied Soul

So how do you overcome the Dark Spiral? My approach is markedly different from other methods for treating addictions.

It's your *soul* that's starving! An addiction is a sign that your soul is empty, hungry for attention and nourishment. You suffer from soul-hunger.

"Soul?" You exclaim. "That sounds like a church sermon or the spiritual emphasis of AA. Certainly nothing new or different! And what does 'soul' have to do with my addiction?"

That's a good question and this book will answer it. My definition of "soul" is connection: connection with self, positive living, others, the world around and beyond us. Having a Satisfied Soul is a connection with life itself. It includes:

- Appreciating your body, emotions, dreams, needs, and wishes
- Delighting in nature, the present moment, and your world
- Bonding and sharing with partners, friends, and family
- Belonging to a community
- Relating to and contributing to a good cause
- Accepting and loving the person you are
- Discovering purpose, passion, and balance in your life
- Experiencing peace as you meditate, pray, or sit quietly in your home
- Connecting with a force, belief, wisdom, or spirit greater than yourself
- Knowing that the world is a safe, nourishing place and there's more than enough of the pie for you

My definition of the Satisfied Soul is comprehensive and all-encompassing. It's your personal belief system, the antidote to the Dark Spiral. Moving into your Satisfied Soul means finding connection in the important areas of your life listed above.

Connection with our Satisfied Soul takes us beyond immediate gratification and day-to-day circumstances. The Satisfied

Soul includes those who believe in a higher power or similar definitions of it, as presented by various religions or the AA model. It also includes those who are on alternative paths and those people who are atheist, agnostic, or have been disillusioned by AA. To release the dysfunctional patterns of an addiction, we need the power and energy of a Satisfied Soul.

Trust me, your Satisfied Soul is within you, even if you can't feel it! The Satisfied Soul is the antidote to the futility of the Dark Spiral. The Satisfied Soul is a space of pure potential, like a field plowed and waiting to be fertilized. Or a piece of ground where you will build your home.

Do you long for more creative and fulfilled living? There's more to life than your consistent cravings. This user-friendly book will help you move from the Dark Spiral of despair to the possibility of a new reality unhampered by your harmful habit. *Do No Harm* cuts to the chase, gives you the answers you're seeking.

Do No Harm helps you develop the following tools for your journey:

- Understanding your harmful habit
- Alleviating guilt and self-blame
- Learning to love yourself
- Discovering your desires, dreams, talents, and capabilities
- Transforming your thoughts, emotions, and behaviors
- Realizing you are not alone
- Freeing yourself from your harmful habit

Understanding Your Harmful Habit

When we struggle with addictions, we have niggling little voices within. Mostly they prompt us to give in to our cravings. At other times they chastise us for succumbing to them. *Do No Harm* offers you both an intellectual and emotional understanding of your addiction worries. Then you can ignore those voices and listen to the callings of your mind, heart, spirit – and gut.

Alleviating Guilt and Self-Blame

The popular misconception of an addiction is that it's disgraceful and you lack willpower and self-discipline. You'll discover that your harmful habit is really a creative coping mechanism for handling past and present difficulties. Does it surprise you that the seeds of your disorder were planted earlier on in life? Coping strategies that later develop into addictions enable people to endure even the most neglected, abandoned, or abused past. Understanding this will enable you to shed the unrelenting angst that's running and ruining your life.

Learning to Love Yourself

When you work on emerging from the Dark Spiral of self-disgust, you'll find you're a loving and worthwhile person. You deserve a life of abundance and prosperity.

Discovering Your Desires, Dreams, Talents, and Capabilities

Letting go of your preoccupation with your harmful habit gives you the space to act upon your needs and wants. You'll find the time and energy to shape your world according to your dreams.

Transforming Your Thoughts, Emotions, and Behavior

Do you believe you have no inner strength or self-discipline? Have you ever asked yourself, "What's wrong with me? Why can't I just kick this dreadful habit that's ruining my life?" Do you feel out of control?

As you'll see in later chapters, quite the opposite is true. When you change your negative emotions and thought patterns, your lifestyle will change for the positive. You'll learn strategies to change your thoughts, feelings, and behavior. You'll be empowered to move from "not enough" to "more than enough."

Realizing You Are Not Alone

Reading about others who have liberated themselves from their addictions helps you break out of the isolation of shame and silence. You are not alone. Feeling isolated and disconnected is a major symptom of addictions. Each chapter in this book presents stories of people who repair their broken relationship with life. My hope is that these stories will help you understand the origins of your own struggle. Like them, you too can win your addiction battle.

Freeing Yourself from Your Harmful Habit

Most of all, this book is geared to help you break those ancient, entrenched patterns that cause you so much anguish. We'll work on changing your belief that you're allowed only a tiny slice of the cake of life. I invite you to embrace the "prosperity principle" – that the whole cake can be yours!

Many of my clients entered therapy because they decided there was more to life than their guilty struggles with addictive substances.

Watching them discover themselves, grow and blossom is intensely rewarding for me. They leave me and step confidently onto the path of a rich and prosperous life. That's when I know

I've had a part in cutting the cords that bound them to their destructive behavior patterns.

My aim is to guide you from the Dark Spiral of despair to the possibility of a new reality. I invite you to end your inner conflicts and take nourishment from the everyday marvels of our planet, and this, *your* life.

> Roberta Meyer is an alcohol abuse educator with a background of teaching young people in schools about alcoholism. She is the author of *The Parent Connection,* a book on communicating with children about the dangers of alcoholism. Her conviction is that alcoholism is a physiological disease such as diabetes. It can hit at any age. Meyer found gratification in her work with people addicted to alcohol because of the high possibility of recovery.
>
> Her definition of alcoholism is that the body and mind feel normal only when the addictive substance is in the system. The person is no longer in control and cannot foresee the consequences of the drinking. This can be the case whether the drinking is daily, weekly, or even monthly. It can be after 60 drinks or even 2. Other predictors are blackouts and memory loss.
>
> Treatment is very individual. Some people can put the cork in the bottle and just stop. Others respond to the AA model. Some need aversion therapy. The precipitating factor for entering treatment is what Meyer calls "tough love." She defines this as the partner, family, or parent setting appropriate boundaries. Meyer refers to Marty Mann, an early female member of AA. Mann wrote a vivid chapter "Women Suffer Too" in *Alcoholics Anonymous,* the Big Book of AA. Mann publicized the idea that alcoholism is less of a moral issue and more of a health issue.

{ 3 }

FEATURES AND FANCIES

IN THIS CHAPTER, we explore the features and characteristics of addiction: denial, incubation, the progression of a harmful habit, and brain changes. Finally, considering certain factors will help you decide whether or not you have an addiction.

Denial

Denial plays a large part in addictions. Terence T. Gorski is an internationally recognized expert on developing community-based teams for responding to alcoholism, drug abuse, violence, and crime. He sees different types of denial. They include minimizing the problem, and blaming others. Or you avoid confronting the addiction by saying, "It's hopeless anyway, so why do anything about it?"

One type of denial is how an addiction is defined. Those who cling to the widespread stereotype of addict – a person who uses is degenerate, panhandles, cannot keep a job – have a hard time recognizing their own addictive behavior. They may insist the addiction doesn't exist, even though others can see the problem: "But my life is good. I have the highest insurance sales rate in my company. I manage my finances. I take out the garbage. How can you possibly accuse me of being a pothead?" This flat-out denial means that the stakes are too high to even recognize the harmful habit.

"They all tell me I'm too thin," protests Celia. "But I love my body just as it is. Last week I put on a pound and my jeans didn't fit. So I jogged an extra three miles and had only water for a couple of days. See how great I look now – I'm OK again!

"So what do you weigh?" I ask her.

"Ninety six pounds."

"And how tall are you?"

"Five feet, eight inches."

Celia is brilliant and beautiful. At least she would be beautiful if her bones didn't jut out so. Or if her body wasn't covered by that thin, fine hair called lanugo. Or if she didn't look strung out and exhausted.

"You're not eating enough." I comment.

"I eat plenty. Healthy stuff."

"Like what?"

"Like lots of salad, veggies, sometimes broiled fish. No meat or carbs or fat."

I hesitate. Celia is a family friend. I don't want to cross boundaries. I'm a specialist in eating disorders. But she's in big trouble. 12% of women with anorexia die. "Celia, you have anorexia. Get into treatment. I'll give you some referrals."

She jumps to her feet, coffee (no cream or sugar) dripping onto the pencil-thin designer jeans.

"You shrinks! Always think you know better!"

Celia stalks out of Max's Coffee Cove.

Do you know you have a problem but cannot quite believe it? With some people, heart-felt acceptance is missing. They can't fathom quitting. Any attempt at treatment is a token gesture, not a commitment. It takes some time before acceptance is fully rooted in the innermost self.

Incubation

The May/June 2013 issue of *The University of Chicago magazine* introduced the term "incubation." Emma Childs, an assistant professor and research associate of the Human Behavioral Pharmacology Laboratory states, "Drug users often form strong positive associations with places where they use cigarettes or drugs." These environmental cues (known as incubation) are often triggers for relapse. Cues could also be photos of people smoking, the scent of smoke, or handling a cigarette or pipe.

Progression of a Harmful Habit

Harmful habits progress from earlier stages to chronic behavior. The earlier the addiction is addressed, the more likely a cure is possible.

1. Obsession
2. Craving
3. Loss of control
4. Tension or anxiety before the behavior
5. Satisfaction, relief, pleasure, or euphoria while experiencing the behavior
6. Guilt and self-blame afterwards
7. Dependence
8. Tolerance and escalation of use (the need to increase the addiction in order to experience a "buzz" or to get high)
9. Withdrawal (unpleasant, alarming, or even fatal symptoms when trying to stop)

Brain Changes

Did you know that harmful habits can eventually change brain structure and operation? Long-lasting changes disrupt the careful mixture of cognitive and emotional functions of normal behavior. Many experts now consider addictions a brain disease.

The brain reward system originates in a group of neurons or brain cells located in the mid brain – the nucleus accumbens or pleasure center. When the neurons are activated, they release the chemical messenger dopamine into the nucleus accumbens.

Any addictive substance or behavior of abuse targets the brain's reward system by flooding the circuit with dopamine. You experience a high. This can happen even if you just *think* about the addiction. Continued use releases two to ten times more dopamine than naturally rewarding behaviors like closeness with loved ones, meditation, a watercolor painting class, or accomplishing 23 laps in the swimming pool. Our brains are not geared to handle the onslaught of our harmful habits. The effect of such a powerful reward motivates us to continue them.

The frontal cortex of the forebrain, the thinking part of the brain, becomes overwhelmed. Rationality and problem solving decrease. Changes occur in areas of the brain that are critical to judgment, decision making, learning, memory, and behavior control. Will power goes out the window. Shrinkage of brain cells can occur.

As you will see in the section on recovery, the brain can be "rewired" to promote health and happiness.

Factors to Consider
- Quality of life
- Degree of harm
- Comorbidity
- Age and addictions
- Sensitivity

Quality of Life

Does the harmful habit interfere with your quality of life? Is it counterproductive or maladaptive to your well-being? Does it undermine your serenity? If it takes over your life, and your thoughts consistently dwell on the next doughnut, bottle of beer, or shot, it's hard to live fully and appreciate the world around you.

Degree of Harm

How dependent are you on an addictive substance or behavior? Do you continue to engage in it despite it causing you trouble; physically, at work, socially, and with relationships? An occasional weekend of self-indulgence may not be harmful.

Comorbidity

Comorbidity is the interaction between the addiction and psychiatric disorders. Depression, anxiety, post-traumatic stress disorder (PTSD), dissociative identity disorder, schizophrenia, bipolar, and borderline personality disorders often co-exist with addictions. In fact, alcohol or drugs are often used to self-medicate the symptoms of depression or anxiety.

Substance abuse has side effects. In the long run, the very symptoms, which were initially numbed or relieved by the abuse, get worse. Substance abuse sharply increases symptoms of mental illness. It can trigger new symptoms. Alcohol and drugs interact with medications such as antidepressants, anti-anxiety pills, and mood stabilizers, making them less effective.

According to reports published in the *Journal of the American Medical Association*:

- Roughly 50% of individuals with severe mental disorders are affected by substance abuse.

- 37% of alcohol users and 53% of drug users had at least one serious mental illness.
- Of all people diagnosed as mentally ill, 29% abuse either alcohol or drugs.

Age and Addictions

The earlier the dependence starts, and the longer it has been in place, the more difficult it is to overcome. The later treatment begins, the longer and more difficult the recovery.

Sensitivity

People metabolize alcohol and other substances in different ways. Some get a buzz after only half a glass of white wine. Others can drink heavily with no apparent effect. Even a small amount can lead to addiction. For some, social drinking eventually leads to heavier and heavier alcohol consumption. This eventually causes serious health and psychological problems. Some ethnic groups are particularly sensitive to alcohol.

Founded by Reef Karim, MD, a board certified psychiatrist and addiction specialist, The Control Center is a comprehensive holistic addiction treatment center.

Shopping addiction is treated at the Control Center. Compared to other addictions, little research or recognition has been given to shopping addiction. Karim sees it as an impulse disorder where the person has a euphoric rush. Shopping soothes anxiety, decreases depression, and numbs out unresolved emotional problems.

Karim looks for a pattern of how the addiction is used. Some people buy only a certain type of item that seems irresistible. Others attempt to satisfy some emotional need by buying anything. Some never even use the items bought. Shopping for a longer time than intended is common.

The percentage of people with shopping addictions has increased with the proliferation of Internet usage. One can buy so easily without even leaving the house. 80% of compulsive shoppers tend to be women. A shopping addiction usually starts in the late teens or early 20's.

Karim finds that it's important to find out why the person's coping methods are so poor. He has an interdisciplinary approach. His clinic uses medication, cognitive behavioral and other types of psychotherapy, as well as psychospiritual methods such as meditation, yoga, and Chinese medicine.

4

A LEGION OF ADDICTIONS

NOW WE EXPLORE the different types of addiction, their signs, symptoms, and effects. As we saw earlier, the Dark Spiral is common with all addictions. Other common elements may include:

- Changes in energy, insomnia
- Difficulty in cutting down or stopping the addiction
- Weight loss or gain, digestive disorders
- Muscle, joint, or back pain
- Stashes of addictive substances in hidden places
- Health problems – minor, serious, or even deadly
- Spending large amounts of time in addiction-related activities
- Withdrawal attempts with unpleasant symptoms
- Rituals like always having three drinks before dinner
- Negative, secretive, inappropriate, or risk-taking behavior
- Unexplained changes in personality, behavior, or attitude
- Using the addiction to cope emotionally and to relieve stress
- Feeling powerless and out of control
- Physical and emotional numbness
- Negative emotional states, mood swings

- Spacing out, difficulty focusing or concentrating
- Euphoria, a high or rush, then remorse
- Guilt, self-hatred, and self-punishment
- Feelings of failure and unworthiness
- Difficulties with self-care and self-love
- Jeopardizing relationships or important social and occupational roles
- Financial or legal consequences

Do No Harm gives less attention to nicotine and caffeine addiction because they are seldom addressed by mental health professionals. They are more accepted by society. Overwork, compulsive exercising, love addiction, and self-mutilation are beyond the scope of this book. They follow the same principles as those addictions listed above and frequently form part of other addictions. People with anorexia frequently cut themselves and over-exercise.

People are often dependent on more than one addictive substance or behavior. A person may be on drugs, drink excessively, and haunt gambling parlors.

When we force ourselves to give up one substance, alcohol for example, we may compensate by dramatically increasing our use of coffee, marijuana, or addictive foods. We may take up cigarette smoking in order to avoid overeating. Then we continue to rely on the addiction to avoid painful withdrawal symptoms. Only when we address the underlying issues, do we begin to heal.

These are the addictions we'll cover:

- Drugs
- Alcohol
- Food
- Gambling
- Sex

- Internet
- Shopping and spending
- Nicotine
- Caffeine

For each addiction you'll see a general introduction with some statistics, a bulleted list of signs and symptoms, then a short description of the effects. A vignette in a box gives you a real-life example of each addiction.

Drug Addiction

Do you think of illegal drugs when you see the word "addiction?" Abuse of prescription drugs, both legally prescribed and obtained through other means, is fast becoming an epidemic. Other than alcohol, the most commonly abused drug in the United States is marijuana, now used medically. This is followed by prescription painkillers, cocaine, opioids, and hallucinogens. Drug abuse is a serious public health problem that affects most communities in some way. Each year drug abuse causes 40 million serious illnesses or injuries among people in the United States.

Did you ever try drugs just out of curiosity? This happens especially with teens. They want to have a good time or improve athletic performance. Friends might be using. Sometimes drugs are used to self-medicate another problem, such as pain, stress, anxiety, or depression. Use doesn't automatically lead to abuse. There is no specific level at which drug use moves from casual to problematic. Although the initial decision to take drugs is voluntary, when brain changes take over, control is lost. Many drugs are used medically. There is controversy over this, especially since painkillers, stimulants and depressants are the most abused prescription drugs in the United States.

Types of drugs

Cannabis: Marijuana (grass, pot, hash, weed) is most widely used as an recreational and street drug for its relaxing properties. It leads to a slightly euphoric feeling and elevates moods. At least one-third of Americans have used marijuana sometime in their lives.

Methamphetamines: These stimulate the central nervous system, increasing confidence and producing wakefulness. The crystal form (crystal meth) is a popular drug, especially with young adults and for those who go to dance clubs and parties.

Opioids: Morphine, codeine, and other narcotic analgesics, both natural and synthetic opiates, depress the central nervous system. Using these drugs makes a person feel warm, drowsy, and content. Opioids such as opium relieve stress, pain and discomfort. Many prescription and over-the-counter medications are opioids. Heroin, processed from morphine, is the most abused and most rapidly acting of the opioids.

Cocaine: This highly addictive stimulant drug produces an intense but short-lived sense of euphoria – a sense of being wide-awake and full of confidence and energy. It's the "caviar of street drugs." This high-priced way of getting high is status-heavy. It's the drug of celebrities, fashion models, and Wall Street traders. Movies like *Blow* and books such as *Killing Pablo* sensationalize cocaine.

Hallucinogens: LSD, PCP, ketamine, angel dust, acid, and ecstasy are stimulants that increase brain activity and produce profound disturbances in the user's perception of reality. Ketamine gives a feeling of mind-body separation.

Inhalants: Aerosols are vasodilators that lower blood pressure and increase the heart rate. It's a sad fact that younger children and teens tend to abuse inhalants because they are cheap and easily accessed. Common household products can be used as inhalants.

Spice: These herbal mixtures produce experiences similar to marijuana. The misperception that Spice products are natural and therefore harmless have increased their popularity. Another selling point is that the chemicals used in Spice are not easily detected in standard drug tests. It's scary that Spice is the illicit drug most used by high-school seniors, second only to marijuana.

Club Drugs: Ketamine, flunitrazepam, and gamma-hydroxybutyrate (GHB) are widely used by teenagers. These drugs are common in marathon all-night or weekend dance parties called "raves." Club drugs enhance social and sensory experience. They increase illusory closeness with others. One of the dangers is that these drugs are also used for drug-induced sexual assaults. They are known as "date-rape drugs."

Signs, Symptoms, and Effects of Drug Use

- Extreme defiance, doing poorly in school or work, withdrawal from responsibilities
- Drug paraphernalia such as unusual pipes, cigarette papers, small weighing scales, stashes of drugs in small packages, cigarette rolling papers
- Paranoid thinking
- Susceptibility to dangerous situations (like rape)
- Disappearance of valuable items or money

The physical effects are dry mouth, dizziness, slurred or rapid speech, and red eyes. Far-reaching consequences are stroke, seizure, liver failure, poor memory, impaired motor skills, and respiratory problems. You might also notice nausea, drowsiness, nasal congestion, or nose bleeds. The pupils of eyes can become larger or smaller. Opioids cause drowsiness, reduce heart rate, and widen blood vessels. They even may depress breathing reflexes.

Long-term effects of heroin and intravenous needle use include infectious diseases such as HIV/AIDS and Hepatitis B and C, bacterial infections, abscesses, infection of heart lining and valves, and arthritis. Death can occur from overdose.

> Jack was my buddy. He and I hung out together. My parents were solemn folks, very serious. Jack's parents were not like mine. They kidded each other, laughed and joked a lot. I spent a weekend at their house when I was fourteen. He and his family smoked pot. Jack asked me if I wanted to try it. At first I was hesitant, but he persuaded me. He told me how great I'd feel. He was right. After the first hit, I was hooked. When I got home, I was anxious and restless, not knowing what was wrong with me. Suddenly I realized that I needed more pot. Each day after school, I went to Jack's for a quick high. Little did I know how much trouble my drug taking would cause me down the road.

Alcohol Addiction

It's not easy to draw the line between social and problem drinking. Drinking is accepted in most cultures. The effects vary widely from person to person. For many experts, alcoholism is not defined by what you drink, when you drink it, or even how much you drink. The bottom line is how alcohol affects you. If your drinking is causing difficulties in your home, social, or work life, you have a drinking problem.

Alcohol abuse generally refers to people who do not display the characteristics of alcoholism, but still have a problem with it. They are not as dependent on alcohol as an alcoholic.

A functional alcoholic can hold large amounts of alcohol without physical effects, but is emotionally dependent on it.

This is the case with Jessy who cannot do without a shot of bourbon (her eye-opener) in her morning coffee.

A standard drink is one can of beer, one glass of wine, or one mixed drink. Distilled spirits or liquors such as brandy, whisky, rum, or arrack have a higher alcoholic content than beer or wine. They are more potent. The term "hard liquor" is used in North America to distinguish distilled beverages from un-distilled or weaker ones.

Some statistics reported by the National Institute on Alcohol Abuse and Alcoholism:

- In 2012, 24.6% of people aged 18 or older reported that they engaged in binge drinking in the past month (five or more alcoholic drinks on the same occasion).
- 7.1% reported that they drank heavily in the past month (five or more drinks on the same occasion).
- Only about 15% of people with an alcohol use disorder ever receive treatment.
- Nearly 85,000 people die from alcohol-related causes each year in the United States. Some say that this is the third leading cause of preventable death in our country.
- Alcohol problems cost the United States $224 billion in 2006. Most of this was from lost productivity but also from health care and property damage costs. These issues affect all Americans, whether or not they drink.

Signs, Symptoms, and Effects of Alcohol Addiction

- Gulping drinks quickly in order to get drunk and feel good
- Larger quantities of alcohol needed to feel its effect
- Sneaking drinks at a party
- Difficulty in decision making, processing emotions, and controlling impulses
- Slurred or rapid speech
- DUIs, exposure to dangerous situations (rape, assault, driving accidents)

- Drastic behavior changes while drinking, such as becoming angry or violent
- Binge drinking (having a six pack of beer or a bottle of wine at one time)

Other affects might be blacking out, forgetting chunks of time, nausea, sweating, shaking, hangovers, drowsiness, or dizziness. More serious or even deadly consequences could be sexual dysfunction, heart disease, high blood pressure, jaundice, liver failure, stroke, or diabetes. Delirium Tremens (DTs) is a severe form of alcohol withdrawal that involves sudden and severe mental or nervous system changes, including seizures.

> "My job's OK," Andy tells me. "I earn an adequate living. But a long time ago I dreamed of being an architect. I spent every spare minute filling notebooks with drawings. Every chance I got, I'd ride into the city and check out the skyscrapers. Then Dad died. I had to leave school to work. So I became a handyman, then a contractor. I lift weights at the fitness center, watch movies with my friends, and baseball on TV. Girls go for me. But I wish I could get excited about something else besides those whiskey and sodas after the day's job's done."
>
> Nursing his Jack Daniel's at the *3 Little Pigs,* Andy recognizes Peter Grey, an architect and old friend of his father's. Andy tells him about his job and the difficulty of earning enough money to go back to school. "I remember your drawings when you were a kid," says Peter. "Some talent there, some real talent! I bet you could get a scholarship – I know of some you could apply for. And there are plenty of on-line courses."
>
> A seed is planted. It takes time for it to take root and sprout. But slowly life blossoms for Andy.

Food Addiction

My eating disorder clients say, "My problem with food is not like drinking or using drugs. Those you can just stop. But you have to eat to live."

Different types of food addictions overlap one another. At the core of all these ills is a preoccupation with food, weight and appearance. A distorted body image (body dysmorphia) and excessive concern about looks and weight are common to all food addictions.

Seiko, a woman with a stunning figure and a mane of silky black hair, says to me over and over again, "I'm so repulsive. What decent man would even glance at me? I turn my mirror to the wall so I don't have to see my hateful body." Her self-hatred is channeled into disgust with her body.

The categories of eating disorders overlap. Many people, including clinicians, classify only anorexia, bulimia, and binge eating as eating disorders. I use "eating disorders" to describe all the difficulties with food and weight.

Yo-Yo or Compulsive Dieting: Cycling between dieting and overeating. And obsession with every current diet, the more way-out the better. Metabolism slows down so it becomes progressively more difficult to lose weight. Statistics show only a 2% to 5% permanent success rate with diets.

Bingeing: Eating huge amounts of food at one time. High carbohydrate and high fat foods such as chocolate, pastries, and junk foods are usually eaten. They boost serotonin, the neurotransmitter that acts as an antidepressant.

Compulsive Overeating: "Grazing" (nibbling or picking at food throughout the day) or large and multiple helpings of heavy, high-calorie foods or saturated fats. This leads to overweight and obesity.

Overweight and Obesity: About half the U.S. population is overweight. According to the American Obesity Association, obesity has increased by 15% in the past decade.

Bulimia: Bingeing followed by purging (self-induced vomiting, usually secretive). Because of the purging, use of diuretics or laxatives, or over-exercising, weight gain is not significant. You may be slightly overweight, perhaps 10 or 20 pounds, but it feels like 100. Bulimia is estimated to affect between 1% and 3% of women at some point in their lives.

Anorexia: An irrational fear of gaining weight, distorted body image, and distorted perception of weight. There are two types of anorexia – bulimic and restricting. The bulimic type includes purging. People with the restricting type severely limit their food intake. Anorexia can become dangerous very quickly, especially with those having both types of the disease. People with anorexia nervosa suppress or ignore their feelings of hunger. Body weight is 30% below normal and the Body Mass Index is 19 or below. People with anorexia often have only 600 – 800 calories each day. Complete self-starvation resulting in death can also happen.

Signs, Symptoms, and Effects of Food Addiction
- Feelings about yourself based on weight
- Losing weight as the main focus in life
- Obsessive self-scrutiny in mirrors ("body checking")
- Bingeing and uncontrolled eating
- Purging
- Nighttime eating, eating when not hungry
- Becoming uncomfortably full or cannot feel hunger or fullness
- "Inhaling" rather than tasting food

Obesity problems include diabetes, high blood pressure and cholesterol levels, stroke, heart failure, sleep apnea, and knee, back, and hip problems. With anorexia, there is an estimated 12% death rate from starvation, suicide, or medical complications such as kidney failure. Metabolic and hormonal complications may delay puberty and menstruation. Electrolyte imbalances, slowed thinking, low blood pressure, and fainting are common. A knowledgeable dentist can tell if someone has bulimia from the loss of tooth enamel and extreme dental decay. Bingeing or purging is followed by relief, then intense shame – a vicious cycle.

One of my clients had deep scars on the backs of her hands from self-induced vomiting. She had to have her large intestine removed because of years of purging.

> It all began in eighth grade – a tough time! I'd developed physically. My periods were very painful. I felt alone and isolated. Mother was occupied with her own problems. She was a compulsive overeater, retreating into the bedroom after fighting with my father. She'd lock the door and eat packet after packet of crème cookies and read romance novels. I, too, began to eat for comfort and gained weight. Being chubby I never was part of the in-crowd. This led me to eat even more. I grew fat. My self-loathing was increased a thousand-fold when my father said, "You don't want to be the size of your mother, do you?" I could see in his face the disgust he felt for her and for me. That made me feel worse about myself. I spent more and more time with the only comforts I knew: candy, chocolate bars, M&Ms, frosted carrot cake, caramel ice cream, chips, and sodas.

Gambling Addiction

Do you remember how you loved playing games as a child? Enjoyment of gameplaying can lead to problems with gambling in adulthood. Gambling, sometimes known as escaping into the "zone," consists of betting on sports, scratch cards, roulette, poker, bingo, slots in a casino, or online. A video lottery terminal (VLT), similar to a slot machine, is a gaming machine that allows gamblers to bet on the outcome of a video game. Today, with smart phones, you can play anywhere you go. You can choose multiple casino games with only one click.

Most states have legalized gambling. It's becoming more and more socially acceptable and a fast growing industry. States depend on lotteries to fill their treasuries. One in two adults buys lottery tickets. According to the National Council on Problem Gambling, an estimated two million adults in the United States meet the criteria for "pathological gambling." Four to six million are considered "problem gamblers." Gambling is an addiction found across economic classes.

The average gambling budget for a trip to a gambling resort is $580. "Gambling for most people is about entertainment, but for gambling addicts, it's about survival," says Timothy Fong, professor of psychiatry at the University of California Los Angeles and co-director of the school's gambling addiction program. "These people aren't at the casino to have fun. They're there to win big – and they won't let a loss stop them." This need to keep playing even when losing, ties into the concept of reward that we discussed earlier.

Harry, 43, was a bank manager. He hit the casino with some friends for a fun night out. It relieved the stress of his demanding job. Then he went on his own, spending hours at a roulette table. He continued playing even when he knew the odds were against him. He found it impossible to "stay off the bet." He lied to his wife, telling her that he was at business meetings. The desire to win was paramount. Eventually, he could not afford to lose. He dipped into his children's college fund to make up for his losses. "Next time I'll win," he convinced himself. He diverted funds from the bank into his own account. When this was discovered, he was charged, arrested, fined, and fired from his job. The financial and emotional wreckage almost destroyed his family's future.

In *Addiction by Design*, Natasha Schull chronicles the nature of gambling addiction. She shows the methods of the gaming industry. Sophisticated technology creates machines that are compelling for players.

Many casinos are now full service resorts, complete with hotels, restaurants, swimming pools, fine dining, a wide variety of entertainment attractions, and shopping. A billboard advertises: "Winning just got closer! A new bus service comes right to your area – your first ride is on us!"

Signs, Symptoms, and Effects of Gambling Addiction

- Losing track of time and space
- Reliving past gambling excursions, planning for future gambling experiences
- Thinking of ways to secure money to finance gambling
- Needing more and more money
- Repeated, unsuccessful attempts to stop or reduce betting behaviors
- Fatigue or irritability due to loss of sleep
- Intensive gambling after losing money in an effort to recoup losses
- Depending on others for money to resolve dire financial situations
- Committing crimes (stealing, fraud, or forgery) to finance gambling

Sexual Addiction

A sexual addiction is a disorder of intimacy and relationship. Sex is not satisfying emotionally. For some, sexual thoughts, fantasies, and acts interfere with work, relationships, and daily functioning. For others, the addiction takes the form of pornography, cybersex, or compulsive masturbation. Sexual masochism or sexual sadism is sexual arousal or excitement resulting from receiving or giving pain, suffering, or humiliation. In its extreme form, a sex addiction involves illegal activities such as voyeurism, exhibitionism, child molestation, obscene phone calls, or even rape.

> I've always had a strong sex drive. I felt lucky that Ron enjoyed sex as much as I did. But only five years after we married, our sex life started to fade away. He would have sex with me only monthly, if that. I was concerned about our diminishing sex life. We also seemed to lose our emotional connection. He became secretive. I wondered if he was having an affair.
>
> One day, I discovered him visiting porn sites on his computer. After he left for work, I looked at the sites. The graphic images shocked and disgusted me. I felt confused and scared. At 3 a.m. one morning I caught him watching porn once more.
>
> When I confronted him, he was outraged: "You're prying into my private time. This is a harmless hobby. Why are you so upset? You're just far too sensitive?" He refused to go to treatment with me until I threatened divorce.

About 70% of those with a sexual addiction report suicidal thoughts and extreme guilt because of their activities. A conservative estimate of statistics from the Society for the Advancement of Sexual Health is that 3% to 5% of the United States' population suffers from sexual compulsion disorders. The estimate is considered low because it is based on those seeking treatment for sex addiction. Many people avoid exposure and cannot be easily tracked. Cybersex is more susceptible to secrecy.

Signs, Symptoms, and Effects of Sexual Addiction

- Preoccupation with sexual fantasies
- Obsessive pursuit of casual sex
- Risk of sexually transmitted diseases
- Compulsive masturbation
- Exhibitionism, voyeurism
- Obsessively dating through personal ads

- Needing pornography to become aroused
- Cybersex, adult chat rooms, or adult fantasy role-play sites
- Affairs, extra-marital sex
- Massage parlors, visiting prostitutes
- Prostitution
- Trading sex for drugs or alcohol
- Sex based on pain
- Exploiting others for sex
- Multiple one-night stands, anonymous sex with strangers
- Many sexual partners

People with a sex addiction have severe marital and relationship problems. Bonding with the sexual partner does not happen. There is a high risk of infecting a spouse with a sexually transmitted disease. Physical effects include HIV (human immunodeficiency virus) infection, AIDS (acquired immune deficiency syndrome), genital herpes, syphilis, and gonorrhea. There could be genital injury or injury resulting from sexual masochism and sadism.

Internet Addiction

A new word, "Webpocalypse," refers to the prevalence of Internet addiction or dependency. This virtual world substitutes for connecting with others and contributes heavily to the other addictions. Spending excessive and nonessential time online is now a major concern. The Internet is all encompassing. We use it for research, to explore resources, access data, and communicate with friends and family. We can study for degrees, pay bills, and make vacation plans. The Internet is accessed from mobile phones as well as from tablets, laptops, and computers.

While easy access to the Internet is essential, it can be a breeding ground for Internet addiction.

Excessive and compulsive Internet use may revolve around on-line chat rooms, pornography, eBay or database searches, social media, texting, mobile phone use, blogging, gambling, gaming, shopping, stock trading, or use of online auction sites. The most common online activities are online gambling, online gaming, cybersex, and cyber-relationship addiction. Approximately 40 million people in the United States use the Internet for sexual stimulation. 25% of all search engine requests are porn-related.

Each type of Internet usage carries its own special reward. With video games, we create a fantasy world. We imagine ourselves as heroes or villains of our own story. We enter a compelling parallel existence, one of our choosing. Then we can defy life's reality and its complications. Online games include arcade events, puzzle games, funny games, sports competitions, tournaments playoffs, shooting matches, and much more.

Cybersex and pornography provide sexual stimulation. A false sense of connection and intimacy is experienced on dating sites and chat rooms. "Sexting" (a portmanteau of "sex" and "texting") is sending sexually explicit messages or photographs, primarily between mobile phones. Both online and through email, romance and friendship are enjoyed without the complications of a real relationship.

Recent studies by Stanford show that:

- 82% of people spent more time online than anticipated.
- 65% of people claimed they use the Internet to escape their problems.
- Approximately one out of every eight Americans have signs of Internet addiction.
- A third of students spend more than unwarranted five hours per day on the Internet.

The average time people with this addiction spend at their computers, apart from necessary studies or work, is 38 hours per week. The Internet impacts other addictions. When was the last time you used the Internet for a purchase? You can buy practically anything without having to go to a store.

Signs, Symptoms, and Effects of Internet Addiction

- Overuse of digital devices
- Preoccupation with Internet activities and the next online session
- Restless or irritable when not online
- Using the Internet as a way of avoiding closeness to others
- Euphoria from spending excessive amounts of time online
- Information overload
- Attempts to conceal nonessential Internet use from family and employers

> Marilyn, age 48, had never been socially inclined. She was amazed by what her new computer could do. She called it "my miracle toy." At first, just a few hours per week were spent scanning a variety of social chat rooms. Eventually she devoted up to 55 hours a week with her computer. "It's a marvel, so much fun. And friendly," she added. Once established in a particular chat room, she discovered a sense of community she'd never before experienced.
>
> Marilyn logged on first thing in the morning. She checked her e-mail again and again throughout the day. Sometimes she'd use the Internet until dawn. She'd become depressed, anxious, and irritable whenever she was not sitting in front of her computer. Buying an android soon fixed that. Now she could access her favorite chat room from coffee houses, parks, and even from the grocery store.

Do you find you're spending more time online and less with friends and family? An effect of Internet addiction is that online friends become more important than real-life relationships.

Withdrawal symptoms can be similar to those experienced by alcohol users. Loneliness and alienation from others is common. Physical consequences are back and neck problems, severe headaches, dry eyes, strained vision, and Carpal Tunnel Syndrome (pain and numbness in hands and wrists). Lack of sleep can have serious physical and emotional repercussions.

Shopping and Spending Addiction

Can you stop yourself from buying something you can't afford? Are you guided by the boundaries of a budget? Or do you find yourself making chronic, repetitive purchases? Many people spend well over their income, causing serious financial trouble.

According to a telephone survey of 2500 adults, more than one in twenty adults nationwide suffer from compulsive buying. Research indicates that between 8% and 10% of Americans are classified as compulsive buyers. *Time* and *Money* magazines report that the average credit card debt for United States citizens is close to $10,000. This mostly comes from unnecessary purchasing.

Social and cultural factors increase our shopping and spending. Our consumer-oriented society encourages us to "shop till we drop." Credit is easily available and on-line shopping is accessible twenty-four hours a day.

According to Donald Black, MD, professor of psychiatry at the University of Iowa College of Medicine, "In America, shopping is embedded in our culture." Compulsive shopping is a seasonal balm for the depression, anxiety and loneliness during the December holiday season.

I had always been the good kid, carefully controlled by my parents, an obedient subject for their rules, wishes, and whims. At college, I was no different. I soon became respected and looked up to by staff and students. I was a straight-A student, president of the student's association, and ran the Phi Beta Cappa. My parents paid for tuition and living expenses but gave me no allowance for incidentals. I had to work as a cashier at Bud's Coffee House. Other students had all the gadgets – but not me!

When I got my first credit card, a hidden part of my personality took over. The card had a 25% interest rate. My dorm filled with the latest in mobile phones, mini androids complete with tiny keyboards, netbooks, tablets, laptops, Bluetooth headsets, and twelve pairs of Fast Trak running shoes with flashing lights. I even splurged on a mountain bike and a Harley. My magical credit card was the answer for all those neat toys. It seemed that someone else, not me, not the good kid, was hitting the Buy Rite Warehouse each day. I'd swipe my card over and over again.

As I look at the mound of purchases overflowing my Student's Union locker and cluttering up my dorm room, I'm amazed.

Signs, Symptoms, and Effects of Shopping and Spending Addiction

- Affected by holiday seasons and the "thrill of the hunt"
- Is compulsive about certain items
- Intends to buy one or two items, comes home with bags and bags of purchases
- Has racks and racks of clothes, never worn, often with the original price tags
- Does not remember buying articles
- Feels a rush of euphoria when spending money
- Is lost without credit cards
- Hides the items bought
- Buys items on credit
- Lies about purchases made or amount of money spent
- Likes to beat the system and find great sales

- Finds solace in possessions

Excessive shopping and spending for unnecessary purchases affect both men and women. Men buy electronic gadgets, tools, books, and compact discs. Women tend to buy clothes, makeup, craft items, and objects for the home. More than one credit card is maxed out, causing obsessive worries about money. This results in an inability to pay bills and huge interest rates on credit cards.

Nicotine Addiction

Have you noticed how many people smoke in the old movie classics? Smoking is not nearly as popular nowadays. Although the numbers of people who smoke are still unacceptably high, there has been a decline of almost 50% since 1965. Many public places now forbid smoking. In 2004, Ireland was the first country to impose a no-smoking rule in the workplace. A year later, researchers found a 17% drop in respiratory issues. Since then, heart disease in Ireland has dropped by 26%. Strokes are down by 32%.

According to the 2010 National Survey on Drug Use and Health, an estimated 69.6 million Americans aged 12 or older use tobacco. Cigarette smoke is one of the leading preventable causes of death in the United States. It contains more than 60 known cancer-causing chemicals. Economically, more than $96 billion of total U.S. healthcare costs each year are due to smoking. Cigarette smoking produces a rapid distribution of nicotine to the brain. Levels peak within ten seconds of inhalation. However, the acute effects of nicotine dissipate quickly. So do the associated feelings of reward. Many smokers realize that their tobacco use is harmful and want to stop. Many try to quit on their own but 85% relapse.

> I am now seven months smoke free. I'm determined to stay that way, even though I absolutely love smoking and miss it. I did quit for three months in my early 30's after developing pneumonia. But I changed from my secretarial job at ABE Health Corporation to Event Communications. My new manager was always on my case. He piled task over task on me, made me supervise an incompetent worker. My hours were long and he refused to pay me overtime. I had an hour's commute each way. Cigarettes helped enormously to reduce my stress.
>
> Then two of my cousins died of cancer. My brother, also a smoker, developed lung cancer. He's now in hospice. That decided me. I already feel cleaner inside, have more energy. People don't bug me any longer to keep my smoke away from them.

Signs, Symptoms, and Effects of Nicotine Addiction

- Deadened sense of taste and smell
- Increased activity of intestines
- Sweating, nausea, and diarrhea
- More saliva and phlegm
- Increased heart rate by 10 to 20 beats per minute
- Increased blood pressure
- Lung diseases, such as emphysema, chronic bronchitis, and cancer

Decreased appetite and lack of hunger are effects of smoking. For this reason, fear of weight gain affects some people's willingness to quit. The sensation, smell, and sight of a cigarette is so pleasing that reaching for another cigarette is hard to resist. The ritual of obtaining, handling, lighting, and inhaling are all associated with the pleasurable effects of smoking. Withdrawal symptoms include drowsiness or trouble sleeping, nightmares, headaches, and problems concentrating.

Caffeine Addiction

Do you share America's love affair with coffee and caffeine? It's a $30 billion industry. Caffeine is a mild painkiller. It reduces headaches and hangovers. For people who need to stay awake for an extended period of time, it maintains alertness. It's also an important element in our social and business life.

There is controversy over whether caffeine is an addiction. "People are hesitant to think of caffeine as a drug of addiction because it doesn't have adverse social consequences associated with our classic drugs of addiction," says Roland Griffiths, a professor in the departments of psychiatry and neuroscience at the John Hopkins School of Medicine. "Yet the basic mechanism by which it hooks people is very much like drug addiction." He claims that studies show that people who drink even one cup of coffee a day can acquire a physical dependence that triggers withdrawal symptoms.

The following statistics from *The Huffington Post* of July 2014 show America's obsession with coffee:

- 31% of coffee drinkers make coffee the most important part of the morning, brewing a cup first before doing anything else.
- 55% of coffee drinkers would rather gain 10 pounds than give up coffee for life.
- Americans consume 400 million cups of coffee per day, equivalent to 146 billion cups of coffee per year.

Signs, Symptoms, and Effects of Caffeine Addiction
- Flushed face
- Muscle twitching
- Nausea and vomiting
- Lethargy and fatigue
- Insomnia
- Severe adrenal stress
- Headaches, dizziness

• Muscle pain and stiffness

Since caffeine is a stimulant to the central nervous system, regular use produces dependence. Too many cups of coffee produce depression and anxiety. Other effects are irritability, difficulty concentrating, and mood disorders.

> A day without coffee would be a day without air. I love coffee's taste, smell and feel. It has to be a good cup of coffee though. Instant won't do it. Neither will cheap supermarket brands. I crave French pressed, Central and South American beans, roasted dark, smooth and full of flavor.

Now we move onto the causes of your harmful habit. There were good reasons you developed it. It was a coping method, a creative way of handling life's difficulties. As we said, understanding the causes will help you to release the shame and blame you probably feel.

> Jackie Holmes, MA, MFT, is the founder and director of the Casa Serena Eating Disorders Program. Casa Serena treats males and females, fourteen years old and up, who suffer from anorexia, bulimia, and binge eating disorders. Holmes has recently seen a disturbing growing trend: people as young as eight and also those in their 50's and 60's, both males and females, and all ethnic and socioeconomic groups now have eating disorders.
> There is still a high level of denial in our culture about the seriousness of eating disorders. There are few viable treatment options. "Even with all the education by eating disorder organizations, we are still looking at a death rate that is the highest of all mental illness. Why is that OK?" asks Holmes.
> When it comes to treatment, therapists, doctors, and other treatment providers are unaware of the various levels of care. Hospitalization is not the only answer. There are many paths to recovery. Good treatment options are available at lower levels of care such as intensive outpatient programs and partial hospital programs. Hospitalization is needed if the client is seriously medically

compromised. Anorexia is often targeted as the only eating disorder. Many people with bulimia or binge eating disorder are not taken seriously. The financial reality is that recovery is long-term and expensive.

The good news is that some programs train professionals to work with eating disorders. Often, the successful therapist has gone through recovery and brings this passion to work. The path of recovery is long and difficult but, in Holmes' experience, complete recovery is hopeful.

CAUSES

5

WHY ME?

DO YOU WONDER WHY you have addiction problems while your supervisor, your wife, and your golfing partner don't? How Tom next door can put away five Buds in a row and you'll end up with a drinking binge after half a bottle? Four factors contribute to addictions: biochemistry and allergies, genetics, a highly sensitive personality (HSP), and being gifted and talented.

Biochemistry and Allergies

Our natural appetites have been altered. Starting in childhood with sugar, a whole range of substances lift us up, calm us down, and make us feel good. Craving sugar can progress to caffeine, alcohol, nicotine, solvents, or drugs. Many addictions are allergy induced. Alcoholics Anonymous refers to alcoholism as an "allergy of the body and an obsession of the mind." Allergy-induced addictions include cravings for high-carbohydrate foods and caffeine in addition to alcohol and drugs.

Joan Mathews-Larson and Mark Mathews wrote "The Role of Allergies in Addictions and Mental Illness" (*2009 Praeger International Collection on Addictions*). They state that people in recovery from alcohol turn instinctively to "allergy-provoking foods" such as grains, sugars, and yeast. These are also the basic ingredients of alcoholic drinks. People with alcohol dependence are often allergic to the grains or yeast from which their favorite whiskey is brewed. This class of foods – wheat, milk, barley and corn – form peptides. Endorphins, the pleasure receptors in the brain, bind to these peptides. This results in a sense of gratification when you have these foods or alcohol.

If you can't moderate your consumption of high calorie foods, it could be because you're allergic to them. Studies indicate that eating junk food can actually change the brain. Do you experience withdrawal symptoms (headaches, dizziness, tiredness, anxiety, or depression) if you stop eating allergy-provoking foods? If your weight is a problem, you could be sensitive or allergic to dairy, sugar, or gluten. Food allergy addiction is the most insidious type of allergy.

The allergy factor causes some people to like strange odors like creosote and gas. That's how they get their fix. Teenagers who sniff glue may be allergic to it. While treatment is necessary, correcting the allergy also helps. Dedicated coffee drinkers may be allergic to the coffee bean or synthetic chemicals used in production. Smokers can be allergic to components of cigarette smoke.

Genetics

Consider your family history. Do people in your family grapple with depression, alcohol abuse or a drug addiction? If so, you may at risk for these problems yourself. You could be predisposed to a harmful habit because of inherited traits in your family. Certain genes increase the likelihood of developing a dependency, even with casual use. The human body contains over 100,000 genes. Genetic information in each cell influences everything – from how you walk and talk to how you respond to the world. The National Institute on Drug Abuse claims that genetic propensity accounts for about half of a person's vulnerability for addiction. Studies of identical twins show that as much as half of an individual's risk of addiction depends on genes.

Genes influence the numbers and types of receptors in our brains. The receptor for dopamine is more active in people addicted to alcohol or cocaine. Dopamine, as we said, is the chemical messenger closely allied to our reward system in our brain. People predisposed to addictions lack sufficient serotonin or dopamine. This drives them to seek the extra stimulation that addictive substances or behaviors provide.

Given a trigger, these genes can activate addictive behavior. Without the trigger, the gene may remain dormant.

Burt's father had inherited his dictatorial personality and his over-use of alcohol from his father. Burt had a hard time growing up. "I was imprisoned by the need to live up to Father's expectations. "I lived in a cage. I could never do my own thing. My father always found something to criticize. And I'd have to be polite and respectful, even when he was yelling insults and slapping me. My mother never defended me. No fair! Luckily Father was often away on business trips. Then I could be my own boss. That's when I got into playing games on my computer." Burt's game of choice was, "War Warriors," a game that has hundreds of players. 16 hours a day he was hooked up to his computer. "Whenever I went online, I'd get high.

I'd log in and I could just feel the excitement flooding me soon as I typed in my password. My real life was nothing. My father treated me like a nothing. But when I sat at my computer, I was a trooper. I was mighty, a fierce fighter in full armor, my lance and club defeating all my foes – especially my father!"

The National Institute on Alcohol Abuse and Alcoholism reports that children of alcoholics are more likely to begin drinking before age 27. They also progress through the stages of alcoholism (from casual use to addiction) more quickly. Children of alcoholics are four to ten times more likely to become alcoholics themselves. This is compared to people with no close relatives who are alcoholics.

Have you inherited an "apple" shaped body with weight concentrated around your stomach? Apple-shaped people have a greater risk of weight-related disorders than those who are "pear-shaped." Here, weight settles around hips. Inherited body types are classified into three groups: ectomorph, mesomorph, and endomorph. The lean and muscular mesomorph is the person we love to hate. Ectomorphs are naturally slight and slender. So perhaps you're an endomorph, born with a slow-moving metabolism. Endomorphs store fat and have difficulty losing weight. Twin, adoption, and family studies indicate that people in the same family have a tendency to put on weight easily.

The Highly Sensitive Personality

Are you easily over-stimulated and react intensely to events and people around you? Do people ask you, "What are you making such a fuss about?" Those of us with addiction problems are sensitive and thin-skinned. We have charged reactions to everything that happens to us, good or bad. Sounds familiar? Addictions help to dull our reactions and escape from overstimulation.

Dr. Elaine Aron, author of *The Highly Sensitive Person,* states that highly sensitive people (HSPs) have a low pain threshold, physically and emotionally. This has a chemical base. She writes: "Having a sensitive nervous system is normal, a basic neural trait. You probably inherited it. It occurs in about 15% to 20% of the population." Aron is at pains to clarify that high sensitivity has often been labeled as derogatory. It's confused with innate shyness, social anxiety, phobia, and fearfulness (labels that have also been applied to people with addictions).

Our fast-moving environment is over-stimulating. No wonder many HSPs self-medicate with addictive behaviors or substances. In his article, "Drug Use as a Protective System," Psychiatrist Leon Wurmser commented: "Anxiety of an over-whelming nature and the emotional feelings of pain, injury, woundedness, and vulnerability appear to be a feature common to all types of compulsive drug use."

Because of this personality trait, HSPs experience extra stress. Stress activates the fight-flight response in the amygda-la, deep in our brain. In response, the amygdala releases adrena-lin and we are overwhelmed by fear, anger, or anxiety.

The addiction protects HSPs from being engulfed or devas-tated by panic. If you're highly sensitive and have clairsentience abilities (feeling others' emotions), crowds or stressful situations can be difficult to cope with. Under the influences of an addic-tive substance or behavior, senses become foggy or euphoric. Then you're spared from dealing with overpowering situations. HSPs are frequently psychic without knowing it. Those who are unaware of this may lack the tools for working with their extra-sensory abilities.

"It is not surprising that artists turn to drugs, alcohol, and medications to control their arousal or to recontact their inner self," Elaine Aron comments. "But the long-term effect is a body further off balance."

Talented, Gifted – and Addicted

HSPs have many positive traits such as creativity, spirituality, and intuition. This is good news! Properly utilized, these traits can pave the way to recovery.

In his article, "Gifted, Talented, Addicted," Douglas Eby of Talent Development Resources quotes Pearl Buck: "The truly creative mind in any field is no more than this: a human creature born abnormally, inhumanly sensitive."

Brian's parents brought him to Timber Cove Recovery Center because of his cocaine addiction. He had been diagnosed with ADHD and mild autism. He could not spell or sit still in class. With the help of tutors and home study, he'd managed to graduate from high school. Now he was in a community college.

Brian confided to his counselor that his greatest wish was to be an architect. He showed her his drawings. His counselor, herself an artist, was amazed. Brian's innovative drawings of buildings were more avant-garde than any building she had ever seen. His paintings of animals were exhibition quality. One day he brought his guitar to a session and treated her to his own compositions.

The counselor acted as an interpreter between Brian and his parents. She translated his "language" of line, space, and melody to the parents – stolid, unimaginative, and conservative citizens whose practical and everyday universe was so different from his. The counselor opened a door for the family. The parents learned to accept and appreciate their son's unique gifts.

Eby adds: "A number of people with exceptional abilities have used drugs and alcohol as self-medication to ease the pain of that sensitivity, or as a way to enhance thinking and creativity. Sometimes they risk addiction." He names many famous artists and composers who have used drugs, alcohol or other substances, including Aldous Huxley, Samuel Taylor Coleridge, Edgar Allen Poe, Fyodor Dostoevsky, Allen Ginsberg, and Beethoven.

Certainly in my practice as a specialist in eating disorders, I find that my clients are exceptionally creative. One aim of therapy is to manifest hidden creative abilities.

Signs and Symptoms of a Highly Sensitive Person
– A Self-Test

Do you:

- Have a low pain threshold, emotionally and physically
- Often feel hurt, rejected, or criticized
- Have a unique way of thinking and perceiving the world
- Feel you don't belong
- Experience other's pain and try to fix it
- Need alone time after busy days
- Have an intense and magical inner life with vivid dreams
- Experience intense reactions to loud sounds, intrusive talking, or people intruding on your space
- Have a sense of joy, wonder, and curiosity about the world
- Respond powerfully to the arts
- Value nonconformity
- Notice subtleties in the world around you
- Respond strongly to sad, violent, or touching circumstances
- Know things without being told
- Enjoy learning
- See yourself as creative, spiritual, and intelligent, with broad and comprehensive thought patterns

If ten or more of these points are true for you, you are probably a HSP. Aron claims that HSPs are indeed "a different breed." Emphasizing the positive aspects of high sensitivity makes it easier to decrease your dependence on harmful habits.

Susceptibility does not mean inevitability. You are not doomed by your past or inherited tendencies! Realizing that your dependence could be metabolic or genetic, rather than a character flaw, can be reassuring.

The old question "nature *or* nurture" is not true for addictions. Rather, it's "nature *and* nurture." Addictions come from the dynamic interaction between genes and the environment.

Many people from addicted families have overcome negative family history. They now live fulfilled and satisfied lives.

Just strengthening your coping skills can make a huge difference in your life. Your genes and your temperament are not your destiny. Use the exercises in the recovery part of this book as a guide for changing your response to events and people.

6

AMERICAN DREAMING

OUR CULTURE FOSTERS ADDICTIONS. Critics of the American Dream claim that economics has become the mark of human achievement. The word "affluenza" ("affluence" and "influenza") refers to the epidemic of stress, overwork, and debt which comes from obsessively pursuing the American Dream. Advertisements tout exotic coffees, alcohol, prescription and over the counter drugs, chocolate-covered donuts, new clones of the cell phone, and other toys as synonymous with the good life. Unfortunately, increasing our material wealth doesn't guarantee a contented life.

Do today's headlines make you anxious? News about war, economic stress, shootings, terrorism, and assault can erode our sense of security. As a nation we're becoming more guarded, more disconnected from our surroundings. We search for something to calm our fears – money, food, drugs, alcohol, one sex partner after another, gadgets, winning the roulette round, or beating the bad guy on the Internet game.

Advertising, Media and Technology

Ads on TV, billboards, the Internet, and in magazines and newspapers bombard us day and night. The late historian David

M. Potter concluded, "Advertising wields a social influence comparable to that of religion and education." UNESCO added, "Advertising employs techniques of intensive persuasion that amount to manipulation." Today's ads not only manipulate but also promote addictions.

Tempting hallmarks of an addiction are everywhere. Can you imagine doing without your TV? The ads portray drinking or spending as the thing to do. Prescription and over-the-counter drugs have become normalized. They are heavily advertised in all the media.

The media holds up unrealistic stereotypes. Women's liberation in the 1960s challenged body stereotypes. But today's media still makes most of the saying: "You cannot be too thin or too rich." Cover stories in magazines catch our eye – "Lose Ten Pounds Without Really Trying!" Eager to try this, do you buy the magazine? As you flip through the pages, can you make it past the recipe for triple chocolate fudge cake? Do you find yourself justifying just this one indulgence?

Are those of us with addictions just following what society tells us to do? I'm not suggesting we go back to gas lamps, horse-drawn carriages, or to a time where bathwater was heated over a wood stove and poured into a tin tub – if you were lucky enough to bathe at all! The rise of technology brought us the wonders of computers and a host of other valuable devices to make our lives healthier, easier and more efficient.

But the scary part is that one of the most accessible tools of our time – the Internet – fuels addictions. It tempts us to plunge into addictive behaviors, from gambling and gaming to sexual stimulation. Teens surf the Internet for graphic information on how to diet, the latest fasting fad, or the most efficient way to vomit up their food. A chat room query was, "Are there any tips or tricks for the proper way to snort cocaine? Any help would be appreciated. Have a good day everybody!" Many people jumped in to answer that question in detail.

Is the Internet your most important companion? Connection, as we saw earlier, is how we define the Satisfied Soul. Mobile phones decrease personal connection between people. Have you ever watched two teens crossing the street together? They're probably chatting to friends on their iPhones rather than to each other. Relationships deteriorate to the point where texting replaces face-to-face interaction.

Consumerism

Do you have to earn more and more to keep up? New gadgets and toys for adults lure us into surrendering our hard-earned money. This ever-increasing bombardment by the media for things to buy is a huge challenge to our physical and mental wellbeing.

Our society works on the principle of "consumption for the sake of consumption rather than consumption for the sake of the fulfillment of human needs," wrote David Kaulemu in his book *The Struggles After the Struggle*. Consumerism and addictions are close relatives. Both attempt to use products and services to "cure" emotional emptiness, and distract us from loneliness, anxiety, or sexual frustration.

> Sally watched, fascinated, as the new casino went up. It was huge, filled three blocks, only a half mile from her house. The children had started grade school, Terry spent long days traveling on his job. Sally needed something to fill the emptiness. With trepidation she approached the casino. A woman wearing a welcome button on her lapel produced a map of the casino, gave Sally coupons for the first game, and showed her around the restaurants, spas, designer shops, and swimming pools.

> Banks of slot machines lined two walls. Piles of bills were won and lost at a throw of the dice.
>
> Sally had no idea craps, poker, blackjack, and roulette could be such fun. Winning, she doubled her bets. Losing, she doubled her bets again to win back all she lost. The rush kept her going. First the housekeeping money went. She borrowed from her mother and sister until they said, "No more." Maxing out credit cards was next. "Just a matter of time until I can pay it back," she thought.
>
> She was seeing her children off to school bus when her phone beeped. The caller was just one of 10 creditors. Sally owed a total of $30,000 on an assortment of credit cards. She quit gambling cold turkey.

The roots of consumerism are economic. In 2011, global spending on prescription drugs topped $954 billion. The United States accounted for almost half of that global pharmaceutical market – $340 billion in annual sales!

Do you find yourself in the vicious cycle of yo-yo dieting? 65 million Americans (and half of all women) are dieting at any one time. As soon as we stop the diet, most of us gain back more weight than when we started. Despite the high failure rates of diets, the diet industry flourishes.

Sharing a drink is a common part of business and social interaction around the world. *Time Magazine* of January 2012 reported that liquor sales rose by 4% in 2011 and continues to increase. Even during recessions, alcohol sales don't suffer.

The increase in addictive substances is partly due to easy accessibility. Use of illicit drugs is declining but abuse of prescription and over-the-counter medications is on the rise. In the *Washington Post* of August 14, 2008, Holly Watt reported, "A growing number of teenagers say it's easier to illegally obtain prescription drugs than to buy beer."

The National Center on Addiction and Substance Abuse at Columbia University asked: "Which is easiest for someone your age to buy: cigarettes, beer, marijuana, or prescription drugs?" 19% of teenagers found it easier to purchase prescription drugs than cigarettes, beer or marijuana, compared with 13% a year ago. A quarter of them said it is easiest to buy marijuana.

Economic profit takes priority over caring for our environment. Global warming, pollution, loss of parks and open space, and the elimination of threatened species of animals and birds are on the increase. As we become out of touch with Mother Nature, our emptiness deepens.

Discrimination

America prides itself on being a democratic nation and the land of the free. However, the prevalence of discrimination plays a large part in addictions. The widely held view is that certain people embody different values from the mainstream. The reality is that those we perceive as different are just like anyone else: spouses, parents, workmates, professionals, children, friends, brothers and sisters. They hold down jobs, have friends, and barbeque in their backyard on weekends. Discrimination promotes addictions among minorities; the lesbian, gay, bisexual, and transgender population; and people who are overweight.

Addicted People

Misconceptions, stigma, and ignorance abound about those who suffer from addictions. They are seen as negative – sensation seeking, risk-taking, and novelty-seeking. Sometimes they are labeled as obsessive and socially inhibited loners. Problems with addiction are confused with innate shyness, social anxiety, phobia, and fearfulness. Health professionals who share the attitudes of our society often think and behave negatively towards addicted people. Substance abuse is one of the socially acceptable targets for public discrimination.

People who are addicted face intolerance and bigotry. Police and crime-related dramas portray them as junkies, dealers, shady informants, the dregs of society. They skulk in dark alleyways, homeless and jobless, robbing the innocent. Those in recovery face discrimination in the workplace, health care, and everyday life. A British study showed that more than 50% of people would not want to live next to a former drug user.

Words such as "junkie" should be as unacceptable as "lunatic" or "psycho." An addiction is often seen as a disease. I prefer the word "illness." An addiction is no more to be despised than cancer or diabetes. Like other illnesses, treatment is necessary and recovery is hopeful. You can still be productive in many areas of life if you're suffering from an addiction. Health, relationships, work, and finances fall apart only in the later stages of addiction.

Minorities

Racial discrimination has a long history and remains a major phenomenon. This is reflected in socioeconomic inequality. Differences in socioeconomic status, greater for black and Hispanic patients, affect drug and alcohol treatment. Compared to 62% of other patients, only half of all black and Hispanic patients who enter publicly funded alcohol treatment programs complete treatment. This is because of unemployment and housing instability. Resources such as counseling and comprehensive treatment centers are not available because of insufficient funding.

A common misperception is that minority groups, particularly blacks and Hispanics, use drugs significantly more than other groups. Data shows little difference in overall use by race and ethnicity.

Do No Harm

Yet drug law enforcement has become a tool for institutionalized racial prejudice. *Dosomething.org*, one of the largest organizations for young people and social change, reports that blacks comprise 13% of the United States' population and 14% of drug users, but 37% of the people arrested for drug-related offenses in America are black. Police are likely to pull over and frisk blacks or Hispanics. In New York City, 80% of the stops made were black people and Hispanics. 85% of those were frisked. This is compared to a mere 8% of people in other ethnic populations.

Lesbians, Gay, Bisexual, Transgender (LGBT)

Internalized homophobia and social stigma create a hostile and stressful social environment for LGBT adults. *Soulforce* is an American social justice and civil rights organization that supports acceptance of lesbian, gay, bisexual, and transgender people. The organization's site maintains: "Some gays, lesbians and bisexuals resort to substances as a means to numb feelings of being different, relieve emotional pain or reduce inhibitions about their sexual feelings. In response to overwhelming oppression and homophobia, many lesbians, gay men, and bisexuals use alcohol and drugs to cope."

Overweight People

Overweight people, primarily women, have to contend with bigotry and intolerance. Geraldine told me that she was driving on the highway when a man in a passing car stuck his head out the window, puffed up his cheeks and yelled, "Fat pig! Go on a diet!" The word "fat" is associated with "self-indulgent," "gross," "dirty," "lazy," "stupid," "undisciplined," "disgusting," "revolting," "unattractive," "sloppy." Overweight women internalize these words.

Weight discrimination is prevalent in the hiring process. In a *Psychology Today* article, Mark Roehling of the Western Michigan University's Haworth College of Business was quoted as saying, "The overweight person is out of the running."

Stigmatizing attitudes towards women with anorexia are prevalent among the general public, medical, and nursing staff. Sufferers deal with comments such as "Men like meat – not bones!"

The Quick Fix

Do you have time to stop and stare? To take a deep breath, marvel at the full moon between the branches of the oak tree, or relish the call of the night owl? Everything moves fast in our society. Distraction is instantaneous – just a click of your android. Addictions are very much part of the quick fix. The glass of beer gets us up in the morning; that joint helps us relax; the morning cup of joe multiplies during our hectic day; doughnuts keep us going when that report is due by end of day; social networking distracts us from the day's stress.

Our harassed doctors are only too happy to write out a prescription. Western medicine is still the rule, rather than the lengthy route of alternative medicine. There is no instantaneous remedy for an addiction. Recovery from habits accumulated over a lifetime needs slow and patient work. The brain needs time to establish new circuits. We need time to change familiar patterns of thought and behavior.

A Spiritual Vacuum in America

It's hard to argue with Al Gore who said, "The accumulation of material goods is at an all-time high, but so is the number of people who feel an emptiness in their lives."

Addictions stem from the Dark Spiral, that sense of emptiness, from soul-hunger. David Myers is the author of *The American Paradox: Spiritual Hunger in an Age of Plenty*. Myer's book explores the paradox between material affluence and "a social recession that imperils children, corrodes civility, and diminishes happiness." America, he says, suffers from a disturbing array of social problems that reflect a deep spiritual poverty.

Our popular culture isn't conducive to spiritual values. Lifestyles have changed – faster-paced, more competitive, and lavish (or poor and war-stricken). They brim with material comforts, overchoice, and complexity. This opposes Eastern philosophy which emphases simplicity. Gandhian principles and values favor a non-materialistic approach to life. Sages such as Krishnamurti extoll minimal lifestyles. In 1854 Thoreau published *Walden*, a reflection on simple living in natural surroundings. Thoreau's term "desperate existence" certainly applies to our world today!

We try to fill our Dark Spiral with drugs, alcohol, risky sex, visits to the casino, computer games, or sugar. The media prompts us to fill our spiritual vacuum with expensive gadgets, bigger and better TVs, mobile phones, designer dresses, and the latest model of automobile. Adlai Stevenson, ambassador to the United Nations, said half a century ago, 'With the supermarket as our temple and the singing commercial as our litany, are we likely to fire the world with an irresistible vision of America's exalted purpose and inspiring way of life?" Our latest "must-haves," leave both our wallets and our souls empty.

Signs and Symptoms of the Vanishing American Dream – A Self-Test

Do you agree with any of the following?

- Ads for diets, alcohol, computer games, casinos, and prescription drugs proliferate.
- The media links addictive substances and behaviors to well-being, glamour, happiness, romance, wealth, youth, and beauty.
- Our role models, the beautiful people on TV and in magazines, are unrealistic.
- Influences in our society make people more susceptible to addictions.
- Overchoice is common.
- Discrimination is a factor in addictions.
- Desire for instant gratification plunges us into debt and alienates us from ourselves, others, and the world around us.
- Material wealth has become the deciding factor of whether a society is highly developed.
- Spiritual values are underplayed in America.

Harva Kendrick, MA, MFT is a psychotherapist in private practice in Danville, California. She specializes in working with binge eating, compulsive overeating, and obesity. She believes the cause of eating disorders in our Western culture is the availability of cheap, plentiful food. Commercials for unhealthy foods – high in sugars, saturated fat, and empty calories – are triggers for unhealthy eating. People who grew up in other cultures and came to the US as adults are inundated by these foods. They rapidly become addicted.

Obesity in the US is a socio-economic issue. Being overweight is not a problem in countries where food is seen as a means of survival. In the US, food is used to pacify or punish. Eating becomes automatic and mindless. These habits persist from one generation to the next. Many use compulsive overeating and bingeing to self-soothe and to relieve boredom, anxiety, or loneliness.

Kendrick begins treatment by looking at the earliest memories of difficulty with food. Did your parents use food inappropriately? Was food withheld or used as a bribe for good behavior? Her psychodynamic approach unearths abuse or neglect issues underlying the disorder. A step-by-step cognitive behavioral approach explores alternate ways of self-soothing. Her clients form new satisfying and fulfilling activities to replace rituals around food.

7

IT'S ALL IN THE FAMILY

Our Culture and Today's Family

I BELIEVE THAT THE PRIMARY cause of addictions is a dysfunctional family unit. Our society underscores the emotionally impoverished and fragile places in the family structure. In both, external influences dictate how we feel about ourselves and the world. When we are unable to honor our inner selfhood, feed our souls, or develop our potential, we turn to harmful habits.

"One of the reasons our society has become such a mess is that we're isolated from each other," said Maggie Kuhn, an American activist who founded the Gray Panthers. Lack of connection and alienation is a symptom of our modern society. Americans on average spend only 40 minutes a week playing with their children. Working couples talk to one another on average only 12 minutes a day.

Since the 1950s, the number of single parent homes has increased to the point of catastrophe. Raising a child is difficult enough in a two-parent home, especially in tough economic conditions. The situation is worse with only one parent. Parents today bring in less income. The result is fewer opportunities for a good education and enriching extra-curricular activities. Trying to make ends meet also takes time – time spent away from children who need a parent's guiding influence. Children then have a higher risk of dangerous sexual behaviors and pregnancies, of drug and alcohol abuse, computer addiction, and eating disorders. This leads to even more disruption in the family.

Are you caught up in the "work-family conflict"? Many of us have a hard time prioritizing family needs over free enterprise values. Joan Williams, at the Center for Worklife Law, at the University of California Hasting College Center for American Progress, found the typical American middle class family works 11 hours a week more in 2006 than in 1979. That's an average of 572 extra hours per year. Reduced time for the family contributes to its disintegration.

Many workers lack high quality, convenient, and subsidized child care; paid sick days; limits on mandatory overtime; the right to request work time flexibility without retaliation; and proportional wages for part time work. To make ends meet, both parents work. A child with overwhelmed parents is a sitting duck for irresponsible marketers. Children's attitudes, beliefs, values and preferences for toys and entertainment influence 600 billion dollars' worth of products and program dollars per year.

Where do today's families find the support they need? The proverb "It takes a village to raise a child" is valid. High mobility because of divorce and job changes affect families. The divorce rate for young couples marrying for the first time is now about 40%. Many children lack the consistency and caring of the extended family, particularly from grandparents. They also lack ongoing relationships with friends, neighbors, and community. The stress of these disruptions and the lack of support contribute to addictions.

The Ideal, Real, or Good-Enough Family

Many Disney movies, TV programs, and Internet ads present the ideal family with smiles as big as piano keyboards. Their arms are lovingly twined around each other. The ideal parents have a loving and confident marriage, outstanding communication skills, and a balanced relationship with money, sex, and intimacy.

Donald Winnicott, English pediatrician and child psychoanalyst, was the pioneer of object relations theory. This theory proposes that relationships are shaped by family experiences during infancy. Winnicott said, "You don't need a perfect parent, but you do need one who is 'good enough.'"

I agree. "Good-enough" parents are unlikely to have a child with an addiction. They're able to give enough quality parenting to raise an emotionally healthy child. The good-enough parents work as a team, not needing their children as crutches to support them. They put effort into fulfilling their children's physical and emotional needs. Good-enough parents have sufficient emotional and financial resources to raise a child. They bond with their children. The children can be themselves. Strong and sturdy roots give the children security. Wings are equally important to allow the children to fly the nest at the right time.

The Addiction Family (ADF)

Unfortunately, we do not live in a world where every child has an ideal or even a good-enough family. Parenting, possibly the most important "profession," is a hit-and-miss affair. We aren't trained for this role. We try our best, but most of us have too many problems of our own to emotionally nourish our children. Also, dysfunctional attitudes passed down from generation to generation guide our behavior.

The initial stages of addiction are established when ADF parents cannot care for themselves and each other. They expect their children to meet unrealistic expectations. The children become guilt-ridden and self-blaming. They perceive them-selves as unworthy and abysmal failures.

Many addictive families have these characteristics: rigid, con-trolling parents, appearances as all-important, lack of communi-cation and openness, and little closeness or unconditional acceptance. ADF families are chaotic, unpredictable, or abusive. There could be other challenges far beyond the control of the ADF.

Rigid, Controlling Parents

Did you grow up with the unstated command, "Do what I say, not what I do"? Did your family follow stereotyped rules and roles? Mother and daughter clean and cook, serve the males first. Father goes to work, mows the lawn, and takes out the garbage. Children with rigid, controlling parents are cast into roles that may remain through adulthood. Examples are the re-bel, the scapegoat, the achiever, the good kid, the baby.

Five-year-old Elba was her mother's best friend. Elba patted her depressed mother on the back as her mother cried on Elba's shoulder. This role reversal started off Elba's codependency. When she grew up, she took care of others. Neglecting her own needs left her empty. She turned to heroin to fill the void.

ADF parents are the supreme authority, with a strong need to control what their child does and becomes. They allow no flexibility – "9 p.m. is bedtime so don't think you can go to the sleepover at Suzy's." No challenges from their children are pos-sible.

Aster showed me her journal. She'd painfully listed her family's rules:

- "Parents are always right."
- "Live up to your parents' expectations."
- "Don't rock the boat."
- "Your only choice is *my* choice."
- "Negotiation is for politicians, not for this family."

Canadian scientists found that obesity rates are about one-third higher in children whose parents used an authoritarian parenting style. This was marked by inflexibility over rules. In a group of more than 37,000 children, these kids were significantly heavier than those whose parents were flexible, discussed behavior limits, and set healthy boundaries.

Appearances as All-Important

To the outside world, ADF parents look like pillars of the community. Father coaches Little League. Mother chairs swim club meetings and bakes chocolate chip cookies for the needy. The parents present the face of integrity and niceness. At home they rule as angry despots. "Mom still makes up these stories my wonderful childhood." Helen wonders, "Did I grow up with a parcel of lies?"

Emphasizing appearances causes a profound disconnect in a child. Children sense a disparity between what is presented to the world and what they see and feel. They do not know what to believe. They lose faith in their own perceptions.

Winnicott's theory of the "False Self" fits this characteristic: "Through this False Self, the infant builds up a false set of relationships, and attains a show of being real. This conceals a barren emptiness behind a facade."

"Mother loved to come to the awards ceremonies and watch me collect medal after medal for my grades," said Jill. "She relished telling friends and relatives about her successful daughter. I was excited at having her happy with me for once. When I'd missed a few lessons because of the flu, I got a 'B' for math, instead of my usual 'A+'. The look she gave me could freeze you in your tracks. She told me I'd let her down and I was a complete failure. For a week she wouldn't speak to me. I could never satisfy her."

Jill's father was a workaholic. She had little contact with him. Neither parent cared what she did, as long as she had good grades at school. At fifteen, she got into a bad crowd. Her new friends praised her for holding her liquor so well. Her drinking escalated because she so much wanted to belong and make them happy.

Lack of Communication and Openness

Members of the ADF do not communicate with one another. "Keep your feelings to yourself" is the unspoken rule. Gillian first heard this when she saw the movie "Bambi." Even now, 66 years later, she can still hear Thumper telling Bambi, "If you can't say something nice, don't say nothin' at all."

When I ask clients what they are feeling, they sadly mutter, "I don't know." They are not aware of their feelings because, as children, they were forbidden to express them. Especially negative feelings. Ian remembers, "Once my mother slapped me across the mouth when I used a bad word. Another time she washed my mouth out with soap. I didn't try again." Ian still binges on M & M's to take away the taste of that memory.

Since feelings cannot be processed, they are disregarded. Eventually they sink below consciousness. Later on, the addiction keeps anger, frustration, grief, or despair out of awareness. Addictions can only subside when we learn to express our distress.

Indirect communication – a frown or a gesture like a shrug of dismissal – is common. The lack of emotional responsiveness is painful for the child. When feelings are ignored, little things become big; big things get minimized.

Did your family talk about problems? Secrets thrive in addictive families: "What happens in the family stays in the family." Barry's mother alternated between buying vodka for his father, and hiding the bottles away. This was never discussed in or outside the family. Secrecy is a big part of addictions. Since Barry was programmed to keep secrets, it was easy for him to later hide the packets and syringes for his drug use.

Little Closeness or Unconditional Acceptance

Bonding (attachment) to dysfunctional parents is incomplete. In the 1940s and 1950s in England, John Bowlby studied children who had spent World War II in institutions. Many were adopted or had been separated from their parents while in hospital. Bowlby's research results formed the basis for "attachment theory" – how children bond or do not bond with their parents. Children in the functional family are securely attached to their parents. The child carries over this positive connection to further relationships. In the ADF, bonding does not happen.

Dysfunctional parents cannot unconditionally accept their children for whom they are. The parents' bumper sticker reads "My child is an honor student" not "My child is a wonderful person."

Chaotic, Unpredictable or Abusive

Stability and consistency are absent in addictive families. Normal routines are interrupted by unexpected or frightening events. A parent who is emotional unstable can blow up suddenly in anger, burst into torrents of tears, withdraw into stony silence, or become violent. When family members yell, cajole, harangue, criticize, plead, get fed up, hit, or bully one another, a child's trust and faith in an orderly and predictable world is challenged. This leads to a turbulent, troubled inner world for the child. Later, the child tries to control this through addictive behaviors or substances.

The Adverse Childhood Experiences study examined 17,000 participants in California's Kaiser Permanente insurance program. The study found a close relationship between severe childhood stress and all types of addictions. Adverse childhood experiences include emotional, physical, and sexual abuse; neglect; a mentally ill, addicted, or incarcerated parent; losing a parent because of illness, death or divorce; or living with domestic violence. The National Institute on Alcohol Abuse and Alcoholism quotes a 2012 study: more than 10% of children in the United States live with a parent with an alcohol problem.

> My parents had separate bedrooms as long as I can remember. Father often came home late. Mother would yell and accuse him of being with other women. Then she'd go to her bedroom to sleep off her nightly helpings of scotch. One evening, I was asleep on the couch in the living room. My father was watching some soft porn on TV. I woke up, watched it with him. I was intrigued and aroused by the nakedness. My father would walk around the house with no clothes on. Sometimes he'd climb into my bath to "play" with me. Sexuality came into my life more and more. I found my father's stack of porn magazines, secretly enjoying them. A group of kids and I did a lot of sex play. I became the leader. We hurt some of the younger kids. At puberty I began regularly watching porn on the Internet. At 13, I lost my virginity. I still find sex comforting and sometimes exhilarating. At other times it scares me.

A common thread exists between sexual abuse and addictions. In my experience with eating disorder patients, I found that 65% to 80% had been sexually abused.

Dr. Gabor Mate, author of *In the Realm of Hungry Ghosts: Close Encounters with Addictions*, believes a major cause of addictions is childhood trauma. 50% to 60% of women and 20% of men in chemical dependency programs report a history of childhood sexual abuse. That number could be as high as 99% if you include people who experienced Post-Traumatic Stress Disorder or other types of childhood trauma.

If a child is abused or neglected, says Mate, the brain does not develop properly. The child cannot learn healthy ways of self-soothing. In adulthood, it's easier to turn to addictive behaviors or substances.

Other Challenges of the ADF

ADF parents are not always controlling, uncaring, neglectful, or abusive. Sometimes a child has unique gifts, challenges, or a very different personality that the parents have a hard time understanding, appreciating, and accepting. Or a child may develop an addiction after traumatic circumstances severely disrupt the family: illness, accident, extensive moving from one home to another, political upheaval or war, poverty, discrimination, single parenthood, divorce, or loss of a parent or grandparent.

The Hungry Mother

Do you believe in the stereotype of the mother? The sanctity of Mother's Day? That all mothers are unlimited wellsprings of love and caring? A woman might plunge into motherhood expecting joy and gratification. But the daily grind of caring for demanding youngsters, shopping, cooking, rides to school, and overseeing homework can leave her drained and frustrated.

Even today, many women follow the family's or culture's expectations that they will marry and have children. Too late they realize that this is a role that does not satisfy them. An addiction develops to compensate for their desire to fulfill their creativity in other ways.

> Edna's problem with compulsive overeating was an outcome of adversity that hit her family. When she was 10, a truck roared through a red light and killed her father. Her mother took in laundry and cleaned houses. She had difficulty supporting the family. They moved from one squalid area to another whenever her mother found another man or a halfway decent job.
>
> Often homeless, they slept beneath freeway overpasses, huddled under filthy discarded blankets, or spent nights in crowded shelters. Edna had vivid memories of her empty stomach and terror of starvation. "Eating is my pleasure and my reward," she said. "I never had quite enough to eat. I dreamed of huge slabs of chocolate, frosted cupcakes, T-bone steaks, double burgers with mounds of fries."

The ADF mother is needy and empty. To a greater or lesser degree, she's unfulfilled. Perhaps she's stuck in a conventional marriage that has little intimacy or companionship. Or she has a hidden desire to study aeronautics or become a brain surgeon. She wants her children to fulfill her, to be a mirror for her, rather than to develop their own sense of selfhood. She violates the children's boundaries and sees them as extensions of herself, like another arm or leg.

At the other end of the spectrum, the mother may be mentally unstable or addicted to food, alcohol, shopping, or drugs. She may neglect or abuse her children physically, emotionally, or sexually. Whatever the reason, she is unable to mother her child adequately. She is like a bucket with a hole in the bottom. Children try their best to fill this bucket and become depleted and empty in the process. As they grow up, an addiction develops as an attempt to either fill their emptiness or deny it.

The Vanishing Father

With today's economic and competitive climate, the ADF father is seldom available for his children. A survey in the late 1980s found that 20% of divorced fathers had not seen their children in the past year. Less than 50% saw their children more than a few times a year.

Bob drew me a picture of his father – a newspaper with legs, just the top of the head showing. "He had so many out of town meetings," Bob complained, "And when he came back home, he went off playing golf. He never even came on vacation with us."

Have you noticed the changing image of fathers? The American Psychological Association reported: "Today's father is no longer always the traditional married breadwinner and disciplinarian in the family. He can be single or married; externally employed or stay at home; gay or straight; an adoptive or stepparent; and a more than capable caregiver than the mother."

Although the biological necessity of mothers cannot be debated, are fathers really necessary? Many say the father's role is one that others – a second mother, partner, stepfather, caregivers, uncles, or aunts – can play. Many grandparents today are raising their grandchildren.

The traditional father in the ADF does have his flaws. Rene's father, the breadwinner, worked hard as a cab driver, twelve hours a day. Exhausted, he left discipline to Rene's mother. Rene's brother was allowed to run wild, destroyed Rene's dollhouse with a hammer, pulled the arms off Rene's prized Raggedy Ann doll, and shattered their mother's grandfather clock. When their mother was not watching, he pinched Rene's arms so hard that they bruised. The mother found it impossible to control him.

Frederick's father, on the other hand, was the over-strict disciplinarian. He insisted that his word was law, no discussion or argument. He belted his son for the slightest misdeed. Mother's favorite phrase was, "Just wait till your father gets home!" Frederick later turned to coke to suppress his rage and feelings of abandonment.

The Vanishing Father fuels drug addiction. The *Journal of Studies on Alcohol, Volume 55 (1994)* reported, "The absence of the father in the home significantly affects the behavior of adolescents and results in the greater use of alcohol and marijuana." Other types of ADF fathers are controlling and often verbally, physically, or sexually abusive. Like the ADF mother, the father is narcissistic, pushing his son to follow in his footsteps. The ADF father can also be very passive, allowing the mother to abuse or neglect the children.

The distinguishing feature of ADF children is that they cannot be themselves. They are guided by external influences and have problems in developing their "Inner Core Self." They feel like failures. They are vastly disappointed in themselves and the world. Caught up in the Dark Spiral, they suffer from soul-starvation. The seeds of addiction are planted.

Signs and Symptoms of the ADF – A Self-Test

Which of these apply to you and your family?

- Parents were controlling, with rigid rules and roles.
- Appearances were all-important.
- You lacked closeness and bonding.
- Your feelings were disregarded.
- You felt powerless, helpless.
- You tried to live up to your parents' expectations.

- Your family had secrets.
- You walked on eggshells.
- Parents were emotionally, sexually, or physically abusive.
- Chaotic incidents, bouts of crying, or explosions of anger happened frequently.
- You were exposed to traumatic circumstances – job loss, poverty, war, extensive moving from one home to another, death in the family, or major illness of a parent, or grandparent.
- Criticism was given, praise or appreciation withheld.
- Either or both parents were unstable, mentally ill, workaholics, or had addictions.
- Parents had no boundaries, looked to you to fulfill their needs.
- Parents were distant and unavailable.

In 1883, Olive Schreiner, a South African author, asked, "Into how little space can a human soul be crushed?" Growing up in the prison of an ADF environment certainly leads to the crushing of souls. It becomes difficult, often impossible, to form satisfactory connections, both inside and outside the family. Craving meaningful connections, children of the ADF become over-susceptible to addictive substances and behaviors to fill the void.

Parents are accountable for their parenting. It's only too easy for us to point fingers. As we move into adulthood we tend to blame our parents for the loss of love. Recovering from an addiction involves growing beyond family conditioning. Remember you came into the world with unique strengths and talents. You've used these to survive a difficult past. The process of healing includes taking responsibility for your misfortune and finding ways to repair it. It's important to identify the difference between your parents' attitudes and your own.

In the recovery part of this book, you'll discover that it's time to travel beyond loss and despair. It's time to reach toward fulfillment. To become the loving parent to yourself.

Dr. Sandra Rasmussen, PhD, RN, LMHC, is a certified addiction specialist

She has counselled people with addictions and their families for 40 years. She is at the Williamsville Wellness Center, in private practice, and on the Graduate Faculty in psychology at Walden University. Rasmussen is the author of *Addiction Treatment: Theory and Practice.* She works with gamblers who want to quit and helps their families cope with gambling's shattering consequences.

The gambling addict is an operational thinker: the means justify the end. Guilt is not a factor. The gambler tends to be fiercely independent and feels entitled – "I am special. I deserve." Defenses are stronger than with most other addictions. Lying is common. Some lies are "whoppers." Anxiety is often diminished at the gaming table. This leads to increasing isolation, not only with computer gambling, but also in the palatial halls of the modern casino. Addicted people cannot stop the momentum of the desire to win. When running out of money they have to find more. Even if it means huge debts or a criminal action.

The population Rasmussen treats is 18 years old and above, from young males to retirees who are lonely because of the loss of a spouse. There are slightly more men in treatment; 46% of gamblers are women.

Rasmussen sees gambling as "an invisible addiction." Family members hear of the financial crisis only when it's beyond repair. Family devastation because of financial or legal consequences is often the precipitating factor for treatment. Seldom is there a self-referral. The first steps in recovery are securing assets and resolving the financial or legal situation. Gambling is now considered an addictive disorder. The recovery goal for people with gambling disorders is abstinence.

8

TWILIGHT SOUNDS

TWILIGHT ECHOES OF GRUELING CHILDHOOD memories sound throughout adulthood. This section of *Do No Harm* analyses how patterns developed in the past are repeated and reinforced in adulthood. We examine disruptions at important developmental states, look at "Imaginary Crimes" and the sense of "Basic Badness" that we mentioned earlier. We'll explore why some of us keep falling into the same addictive hole in the road again and again.

Disruptions at Important Developmental Stages

Can you remember when your life took a turn for the worse? Do you know when your addiction started? Human development goes through predictable stages. Erik Erickson pioneered the study of eight psychosocial phases. Each has a positive or negative result for personality, self-concept, and behavior. Addictions usually originate at these transition phases, although they usually manifest only at puberty or just before.

Infancy: Basic Trust or Mistrust

We first experience security and nourishing contact by being held and fed. This reassures us that the world is a safe place. Did you have good-enough parents or caretakers? If your needs were satisfied enough of the time, basic trust in yourself and hope in the world were established. Are you able to follow your own yellow brick road? Knowing deep inside that it will get you where you need to go? Did you learn to trust yourself and the world? If so, when and how? All the stages are built on this one.

Early Childhood: Autonomy or Shame and Doubt

If you've ever dealt with two-year olds, you'll know how they insist on their own way. Don't you wish you could say "NO!" just like them? Now a child has power, can crawl, then walk. Grab the cookie that used to be out of reach. No more of the humiliating experience of diaper changing. Children whose parents are willing to gradually and reasonably allow them to make their own choices gain confidence in their own abilities and decisions.

Preschool: Initiative or Guilt

The child's world expands and language blossoms. Social skills develop. Do you remember how important friends were at this stage? If your best friend deserted you, it was a world disaster! Then you had to pick yourself up and take the initiative to find new friends. To quote Erikson, "Whether children will leave this stage with their sense of initiative favorably outbalancing their sense of guilt depends largely upon how parents react to their self-initiated activities."

School Age: Industry or Inferiority

Children learn structured rules of behavior at home, at school, and socially. Success (what Erikson calls industry) both at school and socially become important. Think of your school days. There was the in-group and the out-group. Were you in one of the favored cliques? Or did you feel inferior, an outsider?

Bad grades and feeling different contribute to the development of an addiction at a later stage.

Adolescence: Identity or Role Confusion

Adolescence is the prime time to form a sense of identity. So many of my clients enter therapy because they missed out on identity formation during their teen years. They ask me "Who am I?" "Why did I ever marry?" They even ask "Who will I be when I grow up?" Charlotte remembers her embarrassment when her breasts began to grow and the discomfort of her first bra. For no apparent reason she would be up one day and down in the dumps the next. Adolescence is the most common times for an addiction to manifest. Young girls often choose between overeating for comfort or dieting to fit in with the current fashion and their peers.

School relationships are influenced by drug use and abuse. A desire to belong to a group prompts many teens to start smoking, drinking, and experimenting with drugs. Drug abuse in adolescence is a very risky proposition. Even a small degree of an addictive substance can have negative consequences. Once we pass the initial or experimental stage, we may lose control over the addiction. Internet addiction could start at this stage since teens often feel like misfits. They turn to the Internet for comfort, connection, and stimulation.

Young Adulthood: Intimacy or Isolation

Leaving home is difficult. Miguel left Santa Monica, the beach, and his passion for surfing to enter the University of Texas. He missed catching the waves, his surfing pals, even squabbling with his brother and his parents. He hated the bare open spaces, the dry air. He realized he was becoming addicted to Coronas at the student's bar. So he left Texas to start at a Cal State school.

At this time we focus on a vocation. We question our ability to support ourselves. We look for permanent relationships. Did you experience disorientation and loneliness then? Discarding one potential Mr. or Ms. Right after another? Wondering if you *should* have kids just because your sister has that delicious baby? Did you explore careers, trying to find one that fits, that makes enough money?

This is another time when turning to roulette or a series of one-night stands feels less complicated than working hard at a relationship or finding a satisfying career.

Middle Adulthood: Generativity or Stagnation

Generativity is active participation in life. Without meaningful activities, we can slide into apathy and lack of interest in life. Empty nesting is a hard time for women who have devoted their adulthood to raising children. Their lives revolved around helping with homework, talking to teachers, attending Little League and baseball matches, trips to and from school, the market, and birthday parties. Then the children are off to college, often in a distant state. The mothers are disoriented, having to seek new interests, other connections. This stage can also impact a marriage if raising children was the only interest the couple had in common.

Maturity: Ego Integrity or Despair

As we reach maturity, we evaluate efforts and achievements in all areas of our lives. If the previous stages have been completed more or less successfully, the result is wisdom, peace, and satisfaction. We feel content. Or if we feel bitter and resentful about unfulfilled opportunities, we may turn to drugs or alcohol for relief.

> I just had to stop the despair. We'd been married for 40 years. We just lived for each other. Except for visits with the children and grandkids, we had occasional contact with others – just bridge or golf, Before Aiwa had the emphysema, I'd drink only a glass of wine with dinner. Her illness was protracted and painful. She had to be on oxygen. First I nursed her myself. A caregiver came towards the end. Helplessly I watched her slide away from me. I wanted so hard to hold on to her. After the funeral, my drinking escalated. Nights without her warmth beside me were endless. The gin and tonics allowed me to snatch a few hours of rest. Dr. Morioka was one of your old-fashioned doctors, willing to spend time with patients. He'd treated me and Aiwa for years, seen our kids grow up. He showed me colored illustrations of my body's inner organs. He handed out graphic descriptions of liver damage caused by alcohol. He even threw in a guilt trip. Did I want my children to spend their savings taking care of me? And what kind of example was I setting my grandchildren? That's when I went into detox.

Beyond Maturity: The Second Spring

Many people now live longer with better living conditions and health care. What the Chinese call the "Second Spring" (geotranscendence) can be added to Erikson's stages. At 65 to 70 years of age an upswing of passion, creativity, and interest in life can emerge.

When Sheila turned 68, she moved to a retirement village with an abundance of recreational opportunities. She plunged herself into journaling, ceramics, painting, joined a choir, and went on hikes with the trail club. She published her first book. Suddenly her life had a richness and excitement as never before.

Signs and Symptoms of Difficult Developmental Stages – a Self-Test

Which of these do you relate to?

- It's hard to trust yourself, others, and the world.
- Your parents did not allow you to make your own choices.
- You lack confidence in your own abilities.
- You accept others' decisions and opinions rather than your own.
- Trying something new is very scary.
- You seldom speak up for yourself, feel guilty if you do.
- Relationships are thorny.
- Often you feel like a misfit.
- You try extra hard to be good or to please.
- You feel inferior to others.
- During adolescence you began to obsess on weight.
- You were confused or negative about your body.
- You tried smoking, pot, or alcohol at this time.
- Sex was a confusing, upsetting issue for you.
- Peer pressure caused difficulties, still does.
- You give too much and receive too little in a relationship.
- Partners, friends, and colleagues seldom treat you with respect.
- You have a pattern of isolation and avoiding intimacy.
- Throwing yourself into your work is a way of avoiding loneliness.
- You despair about growing old.
- You wonder if life has passed you by.

Imaginary Crimes and Basic Badness

Do you ever feel there is something deeply and irrevocably wrong with you? This is "Basic Badness." The term was coined by Lewis Engel and Tom Ferguson who wrote *Imaginary Crimes.* The book is based on Control Mastery, a method developed by Harold Sampson and Joseph Weis. It emphasizes the significance of unconscious guilt. Basic Badness is guilt that pierces the soul. "As children, we became unconsciously convinced that we were responsible for the sufferings, disappointments, and inadequacies of our parents and siblings. We convict ourselves of 'Imaginary Crimes.'"

Children have little experience of the world. They see themselves at the center of the universe. They unconsciously assume that *they* are responsible for what happens in the family. Being dependent on parents, they can't see anything wrong with parents' behavior. In a good-enough family, parents take responsibility for their actions and own their mistakes. They treat their children with respect. The children soon understand that they are not accountable for the family's ups and downs.

This does not happen in the ADF. The children blame themselves when things go wrong. They create magical and unrealistic concepts about the world. They unconsciously believe they are worthless and irrevocable failures, guilty perpetrators of Imaginary Crimes.

These false (psychogenic) beliefs plunge us into the gloom of the Dark Spiral, heading toward addiction. Guilt, an essential element of a harmful habit, makes us feel like criminals with the FBI on our tails. A destructive cycle of guilt is created. Basic Badness leads to addictions. The addictive behaviors cause more guilt. The hopelessness of Basic Badness increases, becoming a chronic part of the personality. A vital part of recovery is breaking this cycle.

Signs and Symptoms of Basic Badness and Imaginary Crimes – a Self-Test

Do you resonate with any of any these unconscious beliefs?
- If I'm successful, I'll hurt others.
- People will always abandon me.

- I'm not supposed to fulfill myself or be happy or confident.
- I need to sacrifice myself to take care of others.
- It's wrong to stand up for myself.
- I'm responsible for others' feelings or behavior.
- I can't ask for what I need.
- I'm always criticizing myself, blaming myself.
- If I'm happy, relaxed or confident, something bad will happen to me.
- The universe can't provide for my needs.
- I don't deserve good things.
- There's something deeply wrong with me.
- I have to put on a mask so people won't see the real me.
- It's risky to be myself.
- Whatever I do makes no difference to me or to the world.
- I should never have been born.

Derek, my brother, was seven years older than me. We came from a family with alcoholism and bipolar illness. He was the only person who gave me any attention. I adored him. He was an excellent teacher. He was the one who showed me how to fight the waves when we vacationed by the sea. He taught me to ride a bike, trotting with his hand on the saddle behind me until I stopped wobbling. He taught me much that I still use today. When I drive, I hear his voice, "Look five cars before you. Read the road ahead. Be prepared for reckless drivers."

Derek also taught me things about myself that I later learned were lies—things that made me accept his abuse and carry his shame. I was only four years old when he started to molest me. I told no one. I believed the abuse was my fault – there could not possibly be anything wrong with *him*. At 15, I used coke to numb my belief I was sinful. When he died of lung cancer last year, I grieved and I rejoiced.

The Hole in the Road

Imagine you're walking down a road. Suddenly you trip and fall into the hole. It's hard to climb out. The next time on that road, do you watch out for the hole and step around it? Or do you forget and fall into it again?

The "Hole in the Road" is unconsciously repeating ingrained negative patterns learned in the past. Do you leave one bad relationship after another? Or break friendships over and over? Does every promising career prove unsatisfying? If so you're falling into the Hole in the Road, again and again, without realizing it.

Signs and Symptoms of the Hole in the Road – a Self-Test

Do you have any of these symptoms?

- Arriving home exhausted and numb after long hours at a demanding job
- Spending evenings mindlessly watching TV
- Repeatedly leaving jobs, friends, relationships, communities, or living situations
- Lacking a passionate vocation or hobby
- Often bored or frustrated
- Projecting unrealistic expectations onto self and others
- Attracted to toxic people and situations
- Needing constant approval or attention from others to feel good
- Avoiding conflict at all costs
- A backlog of anger erupting unexpectedly
- Feeling lonely, isolated, and abandoned
- Overreacting to situations
- Suicidal thoughts or attempts

To heal, you either fill in the hole or choose a new road. The third section of this book offers practical suggestions and exercises for recovery.

Cali Estes, MSc., Certified Addiction Professional, is a highly sought-after addiction therapist. Estes deals with gambling, drugs, food, and alcohol addictions. People who come to her for gambling addiction are often high-end executives who have to mortgage their houses because of gambling debt. One cause of prescription drug addiction is that doctors overprescribe. Many stay-at-home moms have this addiction. Older clients come to Estes for alcohol rehabilitation.

Teens, who find it too difficult to get alcohol, target heroin. It is relatively cheap, a widely used street drug, and readily available. The high lasts longer than alcohol. Spice has led to a rise in street opium because it is cheaper. The user reaches a high a lot faster. The average age here is 24 to 40 years. For other pills, such as social anxiety medication, the average age is slightly higher, about 35 years.

Estes deals with root causes of the addiction, not only with symptoms. Her coaching is action-focused, interactive and solution-focused. Her therapy creates quick results and positive change in her clients. Her background is a unique blend of psychotherapy, life coaching, and wellness coaching. This allows the client to get to the underlying cause of their issues faster and more safely.

{ 9 }

OUR SECRET SELVES

Dissociation

DO YOU FIND YOURSELF FALLING into your harmful habit without quite knowing what happened? This is dissociation – a major feature of all harmful habits. In this section of the book, we explore dissociation, its characteristics, its nature, and what part it plays in your addictive behavior. Understanding this will help you overcome your cravings.

Do you adapt your style, dress, speech, and manner to various situations and people? Have you ever said "I'm just not myself today?" Dissociation is a type of trance. We detach from our physical surroundings, contemplating or daydreaming. Our mind wanders far away. It happens when listening to music or automatically washing the dishes while thinking of something else. These are examples of a very minor form of dissociation, normal for all of us. Dissociation becomes a problem when it plays a large part in forming and maintaining addictions.

Extreme dissociation is a way to cope with trauma. Childhood abuse, poverty, illness, a natural catastrophe, a serious accident, or the loss of a parent produces intense feelings of insecurity, powerlessness, grief, anger, and terror.

Like war veterans who suffer from major injuries and Post Traumatic Stress Disorder (PTSD), we react with dissociation.

You may be familiar with the sensationalized stories of *Sybil* or *The Three Faces of Eve*. Both women suffered from severe dissociation. Each of Eve's three dissociative states had a distinct and independent personality. Behaviors, speech, identity – and even handwriting – were vastly different in each state.

The Diagnostic and Statistical Manual of Mental Disorders (DSM), the very bulky "bible" for mental health professionals, diagnoses and classifies mental disorders. The manual changed the name "Multiple Personality Disorder" (often confused with schizophrenia) to "Dissociative Identity Disorder (DID)." DID is defined as a "failure to integrate various aspects of identity, memory, and consciousness. Each personality state has a distinct personal history, self-image, and identity, including a separate name."

The DSM's definition of Depersonalization Disorder is also relevant to our discussion: "This disorder is characterized by a feeling of detachment or estrangement from one's self." Other symptoms are severe memory loss, depression, and sudden anger without cause. Flashbacks can be part of this – traumatic memories so vivid they seem to be happening in the present. Viet Nam vets came home traumatized. They'd react to the sound of a car backfiring by kneeling on the curb and shooting an imaginary gun.

As we saw in the section on the family, a high percentage of people with addictions had traumatic childhoods. Their experiences were too threatening for a child to absorb and process. For the protection and survival of the self, these memories were split off from conscious awareness and forgotten. This is done unconsciously through the process of dissociation. The personality splits into different parts, a major factor in addictions.

Then later, when the addiction develops, it too becomes a form of dissociation.

Mild Multiplicity

Dissociation covers a wide range. Some of this, as you saw, is common and normal. An addiction is a milder form of DID, an unconscious and creative way of protection from emotional overwhelm. My term for this condition, "Mild Multiplicity," stands in between the extremes of normalcy and severe dissociation. On a scale of 1 to 10, a common or normal type of dissociation is 1 or 2. DID is 10. Mild Multiplicity ranges between 5 and 8.

People with addictions have detached from those parts of themselves that hold distressing feelings or memories. This is a type of trance, a form of self-hypnosis. The addiction aggravates the dissociation.

Judy Lightstone, a New Zealand psychologist who specializes in trauma psychology, found a relationship between dissociation and compulsive eating. "Dissociation may play a central mechanism in which feelings from past traumatic experiences are projected on the self and disordered eating."

Addictive behaviors are dissociative states where the rational, adult self has actually "left." Another part of the self takes over. Have you ever experienced opening the refrigerator and practically inhaling everything inside? Somewhere inside you, a little voice pipes up. "You're on the double-edged sword of a nighttime eating orgy." Or maybe you reach for your third Budweiser while another part of you protests, "Don't touch that, you'll never be able to stop. The drinking will get out of control again!"

Splitting into parts is a coping mechanism, a creative choice in an arduous situation.

Freud, Eric Berne, and Dissociation

Freud's psychoanalytic theory divided the personality into three interacting parts: Id, Ego, and Superego.

The Id, present at birth, is the primal part of us that wants pleasure and immediate gratification. It knows no laws, obeys no rules, and operates by instinct in response to bodily and emotional needs.

The Ego is the seat of the intellect, responsible for dealing with reality. It is rational, thoughtful, and adept at problem solving. As the negotiator of the self, the Ego tries its best to satisfy the Id within the limits of reason and safety.

The Superego addresses and mediates our moral standards, ideals, and our sense of right and wrong. It forms in response to parents, authority figures, and society.

In the 1960s, Eric Berne wrote *Games People Play*. This groundbreaking book gathered worldwide attention by introducing "Transactional Analysis." Berne classified the Id, Ego, and Superego as the Child, Adult, and Parent Parts. I capitalize these terms are because they are definitions of inner emotional states. They differ from our common usage and definitions of "child," "adult," "parent," and also "part."

The Child Part

The Child is the source of emotions, creativity, fun, spontaneity, and intimacy. In the Child state, we behave, feel and think as we did in childhood. This Part reacts to parents and authority figures.

Young children have little language or experience to process their experience. They are often placed in conflict between their own needs and wants (cuddling, feeding, stimulation, and expressing feelings) and the demands of parents, peers, and the outside world. The result produces negative feelings about the self and the world. We then have the "Conditioned Child" that suppresses feelings in order to be accepted. The "Natural Child," creative, expressive and joyful, goes into hiding under stress. It's important that the Natural Child becomes stronger and a source of pleasure and satisfaction.

The Adult Part

When children learn to crawl and explore their universe, things begin to change. Now they have some control over their world. They pick up objects, taste and feel them. The why and how of life make sense. They gather and process information. They decide what works and what doesn't. Screaming for mother when you've tumbled down the steps makes her come running. Screaming in the market for jelly beans, on the other hand, just doesn't get the desired result. Putting cause and effect to work, the inner Adult comes into being.

The Adult state is like a computer. It processes information and makes decisions. Emotions do not confuse its operation. Objective, rational, capable of problem solving, and in touch with the reality of the situation – that's the Adult.

The Parent Part

In the Parent state, we behave, feel, and think just as our parents or authority figures did. Everything children experience at the hands of their parents is internally recorded. They take in the rules, regulations, the no-no's, the looks of horror or pleasure, the cuddles, and the slaps. The inner Parent internalizes sayings, admonitions, religious outlook, inconsistencies, expressions of gratification or disappointment.

> It was a long workday. No seat for me on the bus. Had to stand all the way home. I'm exhausted. And lonely – Eddie is out of town – again. Before I know it, I'm in the kitchen. Nothing much in the refrigerator. Just a few wilted carrots. The car's at the shop. Can't even hit the market. In the freezer, God be praised, is a packet of Slim Gourmet's Instant Meal. One of their better ones – macaroni and cheese, a comfort classic. Mother would make it often, cheap, quick and easy, satisfying. Again I'm a child, reassured in a home with so little comfort. The Child-self grabs for the box and thrusts it into the microwave. Then there's the good old standby – cereal. The one with the raisins and satisfying full-bodied bran to fill the stomach. Not that weakling low-caloried stuff. Lots of sugar, not artificial sweetener, I want the real thing.
>
> A Critical Parent watches, waits. A predator. Waiting for the right moment to snarl, "FAT!" The word holding a universe of self-condemnation.
>
> Too late. I'm plunged into the eye of the hurricane. Gulping, convulsive swallowing, and frantic shoveling. Truth will out, but not until digestion has plied its course.
>
> My feelings going down, down into an insatiable abyss. Tomorrow morning, the needle on the scale will be the ultimate judge.
>
> Another Part, the rational Adult watches from above, helpless to intervene, "You had that huge lunch at Twenty Towers. You *can't* be hungry! "

The Parent, too, has two parts, the "Good Parent" and the "Critical Parent." Unfortunately, those of us who struggle with addictions are much more familiar with the Critical Parent. Do you recognize your Critical Parent when you take a second shot of Bacardi Rum? Or find yourself at Casey's Casino after you firmly decided never to go there again? You're triggered into addictive behavior without realizing it or being able to stop it.

Do your Parts sometimes disagree? The Conditioned Child and the Critical Parent interact with each other in a destructive cycle. They overwhelm the rational Adult. The Good Parent and Natural Child protest in vain.

Signs and Symptoms of Mild Multiplicity – a Self-Test

Do you experience any of these?

- Detachment or estrangement from yourself
- Feeling like a different person
- Memory loss
- Sudden anger or panic without justified cause
- Flashbacks
- Acting, feeling, and thinking as in childhood
- Childish behavior
- Spacing or trancing out, losing time
- Intrusive thoughts, upsetting visual images
- Body memories (unexplained body pain)
- Distressing nightmares
- Alienation from your body
- Intense irrational fear, anger, or panic

Our Secret Selves

In working with the Mild Multiplicty I found far more Parts than the five Berne describes. I divide them into the Challenging and Affirmative Parts. When dealing with addictions we're governed by the Challenging Parts. Our joyous, nurturing, protective, creative, and rational Affirmative Parts restore balance and health. Here are examples of the various categories of Parts that my patients and I have discovered and given names to over the years.

Challenging Parts

Conditioned Children

Infants: Abandoned One, Hungry Baby, Baby in the Well, Orphan
Wounded Children: Greedy, War Zone Child, Good Kid, Barbie Doll, Pleaser, Black Hole
Angry Children: Rebel, Sick-O, Pirate
Hidden Children: E.T., All Locked Up, Child in a Bubble

Critical Parents

Slave Driver, Goody Two Shoes, Guilt-Trip Mom, Disapproving Dad, Helpless Heap, Mad Monkey Mind

Monsters

Two-headed Green Dragon, Brontosaurus Benny, Money Monster

Affirmative Parts

Adults

Rationalist, Mover and Shaker, Ms. Competence, Problem-Solver

Natural Children

Artist, Explorer, Wow!, Cuddles, Student, Outdoors Freak, Happy-Go-Lucky, Little Anna

Good Parents

Earth Mother, Empress, Wounded Healer, Warrior Knight, Protector, Magician, Emperor

Higher Beings

Angel Michael, Mother Mary, Generatrix, Phoenix, Shechina, Yoda, White Light, Source of All

Our inner Parts reflect family roles, a traumatic time of life, unconscious ideas and beliefs, patterns of thought and behavior, emotional states at a certain ages or times, or reactions to experiences or people.

The Parts within us ignore injunctions from doctors, family, and friends. We're told, "All you need to do is close the refrigerator door and leave the kitchen," or "Just don't buy those six-packs," or "Sell your iPhone and go for a walk." But our rational Adult is not present to follow this advice. In its place is a child scavenging amidst after-war debris. Then the backlash. A Critical Parent steps in to evoke blame. Basic Badness seeps into the soul. We head full-speed for our addiction of choice.

The good news – a benefit comes with dissociation. We can easily slip into the altered states of consciousness necessary for healing methods such as hypnosis or meditation. This will be discussed in the section on recovery. Your inner work is to become aware of the Parts within, how they act out with your harmful habit. Read on. You'll learn ways to discover, name, manage and integrate them.

RECOVERY

DANCING
WITH DEFINITIONS

NOW WE'LL EXPLORE recovery from your harmful habit. First, some definitions, then the process of recovery, stages of change, and the question of relapse. I offer you some treatment options and models. After that, we'll address various aspects of connection – the components of a Satisfied Soul. Each section ends with practical suggestions and exercises to speed you on your way.

Definitions of Recovery

Recovery is not one simple decision – "I'm never going to have another cigarette." Recovery is a series of actions and decisions, a process. Remember Aesop's fable of the tortoise and the hare? The tortoise knows that slow and steady wins the race. So it is with recovery, one moment of decision after another.

Rex Cannon, a neuroscientist and Chief Science Officer at the Brain Treatment Centers of South Florida, defines recovery: "Regaining something, retrieving something previously lost, a return to a previous state of health, prosperity, or equanimity, correcting yourself."

Do any of these definitions strike home for you?

The duration of recovery can be anything from a few months to years. It depends on your motivation, support system, and inner strength. It also depends on the duration and intensity of past abuse. Many people believe that an addiction can be managed, not cured. They say, "I am an alcoholic in recovery" rather than "I am no longer an alcoholic."

My concept of recovery is the Satisfied Soul – connection and harmony with self and the world. We will cover this in detail in later chapters of this book.

Stages of Change

Don't you love the safety and comfort of the familiar? Even if it's unhelpful? Destructive to your well-being? You're not alone. Change is uncomfortable. It can be downright scary. Recovery means going through huge life changes. Change goes through various stages. We can get stuck in any of them before recovery. The *Stages of Change Model* was first developed by two researchers, Prochaska and DiClemente. Here is one of many adaptations of their model:

Precontemplation
- Not believing that life can be improved by a change
- Ignorance is bliss
- Denial
- Not ready to make a change

Contemplation
- Recognition of the problem
- Ending the denial
- Ambivalence
- Teeter-tottering
- On the fence

Preparation

- Accepting responsibility for the addiction
- Reaffirming the need and desire to end your harmful habit
- Gathering information about possible actions
- Tipping the balance in favor of change

Determination

- Committing to make a change
- Making statements such as: "I've got to do something about my overeating" or "This drinking is getting out of control – it has to change"

Action

- Starting therapy, a program, or entering a treatment center
- Changing habits centered around the addiction
- Avoiding bars or casinos, regulating computer time, shunning the massage parlor, shopping malls, and binge buddies

Maintenance

- Continuing behaviors of the action stage
- Taking steps to consolidate the change

Termination

- No longer perceiving cravings as threatening
- Recognizing cravings but not acting on them
- Experiencing cravings as brief and fleeting

Maintenance often fails. We don't prepare for it adequately. We believe the strategies we used to *initiate* the change will be as effective in *continuing* the change. Wounds heal, but the scar may remain. A game of *Transformed Universe* lures us to our laptop. We long for the rush of a craps session. Memories of that silky brunette in the dance hall set our senses tingling. The neon sign over *The Fisherman's Rest* beckons.

But our resolve keeps firm. We take a deep breath, count to ten, and work off temptation in the gym.

Are you in one of the stages of change? If so, which one?

Relapse

Have you ever said, "Oh, no! I thought I'd NEVER give in to my addiction again – now what?" Relapse is difficult to avoid, often inevitable. Periods of relapse sneak up on you without warning. The path to change is always cyclic. So view relapse as just one more stage in the process of change, not a complete failure. Then you're more likely to quickly return to your desired behavior. But when you allow yourself to view relapse as the ultimate disaster, it becomes a self-fulfilling prophesy. You give up your plan and indulge in a binge. "I'll just start again on Monday." (Or next week. Or next year. Or never!)

Relapses are common among those recovering. The National Institute on Alcohol Abuse and Alcoholism claims that 90% of people in recovery will experience one or more relapses during the four years after treatment.

Some believe that a relapse puts an end to recovery. And certainly that could be true for those who have no foundation, support, or inner strength. Carol Bennet, MA, of Family Recovery Solutions asks, "Is relapse part of recovery? Yes and no, depending on who you are talking about. If one has relapsed, learned from their 'slip' and embraced a stronger, more formidable recovery, then the answer is 'yes.' However, if one continues to relapse because they have not made a confident and secure change in their lifestyle, then relapse just becomes an excuse for buying more time before committing to sobriety. Hence, the answer is 'no.'" Relapse can be a temporary setback. The road to recovery involves bumps, pitfalls, and setbacks.

You will experience feelings of failure, disappointment, and frustration. The key to success is to not let these stumbling blocks undermine your self-confidence. Recovery is about progress, not perfection. Gretchen Smith, of the Renovation Biblical Counseling Services, says: "Get back up on the horse when you fall off."

I am confident that relapses will not plunge you into total loss of control. Just because you fell off the wagon during a holiday doesn't mean you're doomed to become chronically addicted. Keep on using the tools we'll discuss in the next section of the book. Carry on fighting the good fight!

Holli Kenley, author of *Mountain Air* says, "After we have come through a period of relapse or regression, it is important to take inventory of the lessons learned and to integrate them into our recovery process."

Treatment

Most drug and alcohol programs start with detoxification and medically managed withdrawal. Detoxification is the process of the body purifying itself. It's designed to manage the acute and potentially dangerous physiological effects of stopping use. This does not address the psychological, social, and behavioral problems. It seldom gives the lasting behavioral changes necessary for recovery. With any type of addiction, in-patient treatment is rarely sufficient. People with severe addiction problems frequently repeat in-patient programs over and over again. Two alternative models for treatment are the medical model and the growing movement called "Harm Reduction."

The Medical Model

This is the traditional Western method of dealing with addiction. Addiction is described as a genetic and environmental disease, irreversible and progressive. It cannot be cured. It can be arrested only by complete abstinence. This model quotes evidence that substance abuse causes irrevocable dependence. People who misuse food, drugs, alcohol, and addictive behaviors are seen as powerless in the face of their addiction.

The medical model is a basic tenet of Alcoholics Anonymous. The requirement for membership is a desire to stop the addictive behavior altogether. The first step for people in a 12-step Program is to admit they are powerless over the addiction. A religious or spiritual element is incorporated. The *Narcotics Anonymous White Booklet* states, "There may be times when freedom (from drugs) can only be achieved by a grim and obstinate willfulness to hang on to abstinence, come hell or high water, until a crisis passes."

> I'm now 71 years old. It's taken me about 60 years to gain peace with food. Not that I enjoy what I have to do. Sometimes I just hate it. I envy those who can tuck into a cherry tart from the Ambrosia Bakery or a hot fudge sundae from Angie's Ice Cream Factory. Or even a warm slice of San Francisco sourdough bread.
>
> I belong to Food Addicts In Recovery Anonymous. It's based on the AA 12-Step program. No sugar; no flour of any kind; avoidance of all binge foods; weighing food before you eat it; a planned, set routine for meals. Meetings three times a week, daily phone calls to other members, regular contact with your sponsor.
>
> The struggle with my weight began in grade school with my first diet. Since then, I've been there, done them all. All the diets and eating plans – OA, Thin Within, Weight Watchers, a protein-sparing fast, the Diet Center. So many I've lost count.

> Acupuncture, diet doctors, psychotherapy, and New Age techniques helped but didn't control my addiction. Three MDs recommended the radical step of gastric bypass surgery – which I refused. Over the years I must have lost and gained at least 3,000 pounds. An average of 50 pounds per year!
>
> Last week Sheila said to me, "I really admire you – sticking with that program. I could never do it, I'd rather die." I told her I had no choice. When you weigh 300 pounds, death is in the cards. Now I'm down to within 10 pounds of a healthy weight. I can live without that ghost over my shoulder condemning me with its relentless cry of "Fat, fat, fat!"

Harm Reduction

The aim of harm reduction is to reduce the harmful habit without demanding complete abstinence. The words "addiction" and "addict" are scrupulously avoided.

The goals for treatment are formulated by the person, not by the program. Harm reduction psychotherapy is a non-12-step based approach. It deals with the ambivalence that many people struggle with when they consider changing their harmful habits.

> Cynthia Hoffman, MA, MFT, is a psychotherapist in private practice. She has extensive experience in working with harm reduction. She offers dynamic and effective harm reduction therapy in both individual and group settings. The emphasis is on utilizing the person's own strengths, coping strategies, and creativity to help themselves.
>
> Hoffman's mentor was Patt Denning, one of the authors of *Over the Influence*. Hoffman says, "I believe in managed use, rather than complete abstinence with no middle way, as advocated by AA. If 100 people began AA today, it is estimated that in five years, only 5 people would still be engaged in the program and sober. What happens to the other 95 people for whom abstinence does not work?"

Harm Reduction is a compassionate, non-judgmental approach that meets clients where they are, empowering them to take control. It's holistic and humane, respectful and effective, not punitive or shaming. It does not demonize the use of alcohol and drugs.

I consider both the medical model and harm reduction to be valid, depending on the person involved. Some substance abuse experts find shades of grey. Some make a distinction between alcohol abuse and alcoholism (also called alcohol dependence). Unlike those with alcoholism, alcohol abusers have some ability to set limits on their drinking.

Treatment Modalities

Programs and approaches to addiction treatment differ widely. They continue to evolve and diversify. Many programs today do not fit neatly into the traditional addiction treatment classifications.

- *Pharmacotherapy*: This is medically managed, administered by a physician in an inpatient or outpatient setting. Withdrawal from opioids, benzodiazepines, alcohol, nicotine, barbiturates, and other sedatives has unpleasant or even fatal side effects. Detoxification is often managed with medications. Nicotine replacement therapy is another medically managed therapy.
- *Dual diagnosis*: This is for people with an addiction who also suffer from mental illness. It requires highly specialized treatment facilities.
- *Residential treatment facilities*: These can be long-term or short-term. Patients live at the center.
- *Outpatient treatment facilities*: Patients live at home and go to the center for treatment.
- *Group therapy*: These are therapy groups, self-help groups, and groups that use the AA model.
- *Psychotherapy*: There are two broad categories of psychotherapy. Cognitive-behavioral therapy helps patients to understand thoughts and feelings influencing behavior.

Psychoanalytic or psychodynamic therapy explores the influence of the unconscious mind. It offers insight and looks closely at childhood experiences. Often the two categories are combined. Some therapies tend to be brief while others are long term. There is now an extensive range of psychotherapy theories and modalities. Most therapists and programs are very eclectic. Many therapists and programs utilize trance methods such as visualization, hypnotherapy, and Eye Movement Desensitization and Reprocessing (EMDR). Art, dreamwork, writing, and sandplay therapies are useful for treating addictions. The practice of mindfulness, an important aspect of Buddhism, is frequently used.

- *Self-help*: More and more therapists are encouraging clients to do "homework" exercises in addition to regular therapy sessions. This cuts down the length of the therapy. It empowers the client to become more self-sufficient.

- *Coaching:* This uses the art and science of psychology in practical down-to-earth ways.

- *Holistic healing:* This is also known as a psychospiritual, transpersonal, or energetic healing system. The entire being is treated – mind, body, emotions, and spirit. Holistic systems were rediscovered from the wisdom of ancient cultures for use in modern times. They were formerly regarded as "way out" or "new age." Extensive and results-oriented studies now prove them to be an important part of addiction recovery. Many holistic healing methods utilize body-oriented or somatic therapies. The following are now slowly emerging into the mainstream: Emotional Freedom Technique, Neuro-Linguistic Programming, Tapas Acupressure Technique, homeopathy, Chinese medicine, massage, acupuncture, acupressure, therapeutic body work, yoga, qigong, and other types of movement therapies. Reiki, meditation, self-hypnosis, past life regression, and chakra clearing and balancing may be included.

As you will see in the following chapters, my approach to healing addictions is both eclectic and holistic. It's based on the theoretical material in previous sections of the book.

{ 11 }

EXCAVATING
OUR SECRET SELVES

EARLIER IN THE BOOK we discussed dissociation and its impact on addictions. Here are some powerful methods for resolving dissociation and bringing those lost and secret Parts to consciousness:

- Finding and naming the Parts
- Accepting your Parts
- Connecting with the Affirmative Parts
- Confronting the Challenging Parts
- Dialoging and negotiating with the Parts
- Integrating the Parts

Finding and Naming the Parts

Do you feel tension in your shoulders, overwhelming feelings, and a driving need for your harmful habit? Do you sometimes wonder if something (or someone) takes over? These are clues that a certain Part is triggered. Parts pop up unexpectedly, plunging you into the knee-jerk activity with speed, a shot of brandy, or a stint of *Mediaeval Madness* on the Internet. The trick is to find out what, or rather, who is controlling you.

Naming your Parts is a potent process, conferring identity and individualization. Writer Ursula Le Guin says, "The true name is like a jewel at the bottom of a dry well."

Because the Parts hide out in your unconscious, a visual or auditory aid can help. I ask patients to imagine the Part that's causing them trouble then describe it. Sometimes they see no more than a dark color, a swirl of fog, or a black hole. Other times they recall a sound. Pinpointing Parts and naming them gives them a handle to grab onto.

To Find and Name Your Parts:

- Study pictures from magazines, TV, Internet, and the news. A popular film star embodies an impossible ideal of thinness. A political figure you named the Manipulator describes the Part that tricks you into yet another visit to your pot dealer.
- Find images from stories, fairy tales, nursery rhymes, and folk lore, e.g., Glinda the Good Witch, Henny-Penny.
- Consider movie characters, e.g., Lion King, Yoda, or E.T.
- Visualize the Part that's causing trouble and describe it: Pleaser, Fog, Volcano. It could be a sound, taste, taste, or touch as well.
- To make this more personal, consider giving your Child Part the diminutive of your name, e.g., Little Tula, Baby Celia, or a pet name like Sweetie.
- Draw a Part or write about it in your journal.
- Consider people you know. One of Diane's Parts – The Harpy – was named after her angry, constantly shrieking mother.

Accepting Your Parts

It's hard to accept your Parts because it means allowing yourself to feel pain, rage, or grief. You might very well want them to just go away, so you can forget them. But that's what you've already tried.

You've buried them under the layers of your harmful habit. You know that didn't work! Your Parts comprise the person you are. Denying and struggling against them doesn't help. What they need is compassion. If your Wounded Children within you were *real* children, how you would take care of them?

Beulah's parents were killed in a plane crash. She was sent to live with an aunt she'd never met. She called that confused and disoriented little girl Part of her, "The Waif." My training and experience as a therapist taught me not to shock easily. But Beulah threw me by exclaiming, "I wish 'The Waif' was dead! She makes me so wretched. Then I can't stop crying. So I down a couple of glasses of Jim Bean to feel better." After Beulah told me that, our therapy focused on accepting and comforting the Waif.

Connecting with the Affirmative Parts

Your goal is to strengthen your Good Parent, Adult, and Natural Child. They are only too often overwhelmed by the Challenging Parts. Consider the achievements in your life. Remember how you made it through school, got yourself a job, found a loving partner. Focus on your strong, caring, and good qualities. Think about your friends. Like Jane, who always has a shoulder for you to cry on. And what about Kado, whose hugs feel so good?

Your Natural Children are your allies. It's important to connect with them. Run in the surf, marvel at intricate pieces of driftwood, peer into tide pools, rejoice when hummingbirds come to your feeder. Respond to the joy, aliveness, and creativity your Natural Child holds for you. Writers, musicians, and artists use the Natural Child's creativity and curiosity to produce their works.

Listen to the sane, sensible voice of your Adult. Let it solve problems for you. Allow it to find a remedy for your black moods and constant anxiety. Appreciate its contribution to your well-being.

Confronting the Challenging Parts

Your Challenging Parts evolved out of your fear, grief, and a need to protect yourself. Rethink your Critical Parent. Adjust it to serve, rather than hinder you. For instance, your Slave Driver could motivate you to finally make the decision to buy that new house. It finds the right realtor and the financial means. Tone down and soften the Critical Parent's commands. It can give you good advice. Cassie could never keep friends. She blamed them for deserting her. Her Critical Parent pointed out that she tended to boast about herself and seldom listened to others. She changed that behavior and discovered a new ability to form friendships.

Dialoguing and Negotiating with the Parts

When Affirmative Parts are brought to light, they can keep the Challenging Parts in line. Dialogue with the Parts that prompt you to flee into your addiction. A dialogue between your Critical Parent and your Adult might go like this:

Critical Parent: "Look at how you blew that presentation at the company dinner last night. You missed at least three major points. Just wait till tomorrow– you're going to get fired!"

Adult: "Let's leave out the judgment. That dinner was in my honor! Being fired is a non-issue. Didn't you notice? The chief applauded my presentation. He even promised a raise."

An intense reaction to a situation is your red flag that a certain Part has been triggered. Instead of acting out with addictive behavior, regroup with deep breathing and a relaxation exercise. Take a time out to assess your course of action when a Challenging Part pushes you. Consider which Part has been activated. Bring in your Adult to reason with it. Your Good Parent could soothe it with a cup of your favorite (decaf) tea. Your Natural Child might advise a nap, a walk in the park, or a cuddle with Cocoa, your Cocker Spaniel.

Good parenting of your inner Children is giving love and understanding. It's also setting boundaries and limits. Just like real children, your inner Children need discipline. You'd never let your kid or grandkid grab all the Kit Kats in the market, would you? When your inner Conditioned Child starts whining for a third glass of Riesling, or a meeting with your old coke buddies, tell it firmly and gently that this behavior is no longer an option. Offer it some healthy alternatives.

Integrating the Parts

Each Part represents an aspect of you. It was developed for a good reason. It deserves your love, compassion, and understanding. The Parts need to come together so you can see the whole picture, the light and the dark. It's like gathering threads of different color and weaving them into a tapestry. Or piecing together a puzzle that was carelessly dropped and scattered over the floor.

Connecting with the "people" inside you enables you to love yourself, Parts and all. This is an important aspect of overcoming the tangles with your harmful habit.

"I get sky-high at sales," confessed Trudy. "I call this Part my Money Monster. It's big and green. It has dollar signs for eyes. They flash on and off whenever I pass a Macy's. Its favorite foods are the bills in my wallet. It gobbles up my five credit cards whenever I hit the clothes outlets. Once I get home and see how much I've spent, I'm ashamed and embarrassed."

Trudy hid the items to conceal her shopping addiction. She'd hide them in the trunk of her car, the attic, the storage room, or at the back of her closet. Sometimes she spent a whole day shopping for clothes. After suffering from buyer's remorse, she'd return them. The next day she would go back to the stores to buy them once again.

"I guess you might call me a 'shopaholic.' I can never get enough of the clothes I crave but don't need. I have to figure out what it is I'm really looking for. Perhaps it's not those items in the shopping cart. My Adult could tame that Money Monster. Maybe it would settle for balancing my checkbook and getting a budget off the ground!"

{ 12 }

TEAR SOUP
AND HAPPINESS

DO YOU SWING BETWEEN feeling sad, angry, hurt, anxious, or guilty? Negative emotions play a large role in addictions. This chapter deals with emotions. They're difficult to put into words. They surprise us with their intensity and power. The word "emotion" comes from the Latin "emovere" which means "to move." Have you ever been "moved" by a friend's divorce, a son's graduation, or a squirrel hit by a car?

Addictions are protective. They help us avoid those uncomfortable emotions. Your preoccupation with your smart phone, hash, multiple sex partners, or upping the stakes at the gaming club feels far safer than being overwhelmed with intense, out-of-control emotional states.

We're Highly Sensitive People. During childhood it was impossible to shield ourselves from our family's toxicity. The "musts," "oughts," and "shoulds" that parents, peers, and the media drummed into us were in conflict with our desires. We tried to escape our pain. Our needs and wants became gray, dull, and hard to identify. We communicate and express ourselves through the addictive behavior.

Addictions and Communication

You had, and perhaps still have, no place to share your distress, your anger, and your need to assert yourself. It's still hard to express yourself in an authentic and powerful way – or even feel your feelings. Instead, the addiction communicates your dreams, tragedies, hopes, and fears in its own special language. Inhaling a popper, downing a fifth beer, the hours spent on surfing the net numb out longing or confusion.

The addiction hides skeletons in the cupboard and tells your story. So it's vital for you to understand, translate, and express its enigmatic language.

Which of these feelings and beliefs might your harmful habit be expressing?

- "I'm a failure."
- "I must be in control."
- "I'm a loser – lazy, stupid, and undisciplined."
- "I want closeness but know it won't last."
- "I don't know who I am."

"I'm a failure."

Your belief in your Basic Badness is a symptom of the Dark Spiral. You prove to yourself that you're a failure by going down the slippery slope of addiction. The ADF makes children feel incompetent and inadequate. We take to heart the media's message – of wealthy, beautiful, airbrushed couples holding hands on a beach at sunset. We know we cannot match up to them.

> Gregory was a lawyer with a thriving practice. His colleagues respected him. Clients appreciated his hard work on their behalf. But Gregory felt like an impostor. Although his father died ten years ago, Gregory still wrestled with his father's ghost.

"Nothing is ever enough" and "try harder" were his father's regular statements. No achievement was worthwhile. Not even the law degree from Stanford.

Liquor, Gregory found, pushed down his hidden feelings of fear, anger with his father, and guilt. His drinking escalated from a glass of Chardonnay at dinner to pre-dinner scotches and vodkas before bedtime. He'd start his day with two glasses of red wine. The drinking affected his law practice. He lost four well-paying, high-end executive clients. His partners avoided his eyes when he met them in the corridors. Colleagues gave excuses when he asked them to lunch. After fumbling through a client's defense at court, he went into treatment.

"I must be in control."

Control issues are common with addictions. The ADF was unpredictable, unable to teach you how to achieve inner stability. You never knew when there might be yelling, hitting, or waiting in vain for mother to pick you up from school. The addiction is a ritual, like always hitting the bar or the casino after work. It is a method of keeping order, the only constant in a chaotic world of feelings. One of the paths to healing is to develop healthy routines to substitute for the addiction ritual.

"I'm a loser – lazy, stupid, and undisciplined."

These were epithets applied to you verbally or non-verbally. You applied them to yourself. You did not cause your harmful habit. Do you still blame yourself, beat yourself up? Do you still believe in your Basic Badness? Unhappy with the very person you are? Your harmful habit becomes an object of scorn to reflect your lack of self-love. Later exercises in this book will guide you into loving and appreciating yourself.

"I want closeness but know it won't last."

We grew up without intimacy or unconditional acceptance. We do not believe that closeness will continue, or even that it exists. We fear letting down our guard to allow affection. Choosing partners or friends who are unable to handle closeness is how we protect ourselves. Marcia had a problem with intimacy. In a hypnotherapy session, she visualized living alone in a castle. It had a moat and a drawbridge that she could pull up if enemies drew near. Slits in the high stone walls protected her from spears and arrows.

"I don't know who I am."

This is the age-old identity question. Other versions are: "What do I really want?" "Why am I on this planet?" "What is my life all about?" "What is its meaning and purpose?" "Who do I want to be?"

If you've come far enough to ask these questions, you've come a long way! You're now challenging the rigid rules, expectations, and roles that your family, society, and your peers imposed on you. In asking and answering these vital questions, you're discovering, validating, and affirming yourself.

Levels of Emotion

Emotional states influence your relationship with yourself, the world and the addiction. I divide them into three interrelated levels.

- Level 1: Anxiety and depression
- Level 2: Guilt, love, grief, anger, and joy
- Level 3: Fear, rage, and pleasure

Level 1 emotions are on the surface. Level 2 are more unconscious and harder to process. Level 3 emotions are the most deeply embedded in the unconscious, the brain, and the body. We range through all three levels without thinking. Grasping how emotions operate helps to free yourself from negativity and your harmful habit.

Level 1: *Anxiety and Depression*

These are surface or "cover up" feelings. Like the addiction, they take away the negative emotions and memories of Levels 2 and 3. I call the anxiety Part the "Mad Monkey Mind." It swings endlessly from tree to tree, disrupting your peace (especially at 3 a.m. when you're vainly trying to get back to sleep!) It also tends to catastrophize, plunging you into the worst possible scenario.

Here's the Mad Monkey Mind in action:

- "Of course she'll never love me – look what a creep I am."
- "I'll never find a partner."
- "Then I'll be alone for the rest of my life."
- "This report I'm writing won't ever get done."
- "My boss hates me."
- "I'm going to get fired."
- "Then I'll be starving and homeless forever."

Depression is "to depress" – to unconsciously push down disturbingly intense emotions, thoughts, or memories. Winston Churchill called depression his "Black Dog." Depression is marked by apathy, exhaustion, meaninglessness, hopelessness. Do you experience that leaden state of joylessness?

Level 2: *Guilt, Love, Grief, Anger, and Joy*

We're aware of those feelings, but puzzled about their origin. Without quite knowing what happens, we tumble into them. An ongoing situation such as a long struggle with a bad relationship, illness, or a downturn in our financial situation can keep us mired in difficult emotions.

Guilt is appropriate when it prods our conscience to do the right thing. Unconscious guilt, Basic Badness, plunges us down the Dark Spiral. A vicious cycle is created. We use the addiction to thrust away the guilt, then feel guilty about the addictive behavior.

Love may be defined as holding, caring, careful listening, respect, attention, and understanding. Carl Ransom Rogers was an influential American psychologist, a founder of the humanistic (or client-centered) approach to psychology. He used the term, "unconditional positive regard." You're loved for who you are, not just because you've picked up your room or scored top grades in math.

Love is a basic need. Its loss can be life-threatening. In the 1930s, René Spitz, a Hungarian psychiatrist and psychoanalyst, introduced the term "hospitalism." He studied institutionalized infants. Their symptoms included delayed physical development, perceptual-motor skills, and language. Some babies even wasted away and died. We now understand that this wasting disease can be caused by lack of cuddling and comfort by caregivers. This notion was later expanded to refer to severe and lasting maternal deprivation.

Grief is a reaction to loss of love. It's associated with abandonment. All that makes life worth living leaves us. No wonder there is such an emphasis on falling in love and the happiness-ever-after myth. Most of us have suffered some grief and loss in that area. Your ADF parents loved you in a limited way, as best they could. It was not enough. You almost certainly did not receive the amount of caring you so desperately needed.

Anger is also a reaction to a loss of love. It's a difficult emotion for many of us. It's not a "nice" emotion. It has a bad reputation. Anger is especially challenging if a parent yelled or hit. Like fire, anger can be destructive, decimating a forest. Or comforting and warming as we tell stories, and toast marshmallows around a campfire.

Expressing your anger was a "no-no" in the ADF. Do you still stuff it away? Or vent it on that driver who cut you off on the freeway? Discard this outdated family pattern. Gather up your courage to turn anger into healthy assertiveness. Ask your supervisor for that paid vacation she promised. Tell your neighbor that blasting rap music disturbs your afternoon nap.

Joy is a cuddly puppy, a new grandchild, a birthday party. Like its twin, happiness, joy is difficult to sustain. Peace and contentment have longer staying power. Savor the little things to escape the prison of dysfunctional habits; a sunset turning the Mount Diablo rosy, a good night's sleep, the touch of a child's hand. A major part of self-care is repairing childhood wounds. To heal an addiction, the ancient destructive pattern of emotional scarcity needs to change,

Level 2 emotions are a milder and more civilized version of Level 3's primitive emotions.

Level 3: *Fear, Rage and Pleasure*

These emotions are intense, primordial, and challenging. They are deeply embedded in the unconscious and experienced in the body. The "reptile brain" or diencephalon is the most ancient part of the brain. It was around when we were taking cover from cave lions in paleolithic times. Like our Child Parts, it responds powerfully and spontaneously to circumstances.

Harmless situations can trigger traumatic memories, intense emotional responses. Georgia was raped by a bearded stranger when she was 13. Until recovery, if she saw an unfamiliar man with a beard walking down the street, she'd be overcome by terror. She'd turn and run.

A part of the diencephalon is the hypothalamus, a small cone-shaped structure deep in the brain. It regulates primal drive states and Level 3 emotions. It also controls the autonomic nervous system. When aroused by a threatening situation, the autonomic nervous system is hardwired into preparing us for "flight-or-fight" – for fleeing or attacking our enemy. Fear, experienced as terror, becomes the primary emotion. This was (and still is) critical for survival. It is predominant in any abusive or dangerous situation, especially when we were children, unable to defend ourselves. When we are fearful, the autonomic nervous system dilates the blood vessels in large muscles, constricts the blood vessels in the rest of the body, narrows the bronchial tubes, and stimulates the activity of the intestines. With your body in such a chaotic state – cold hands, shallow breathing, and a churning stomach – no wonder that checking your emails for the fiftieth time that morning, or heading for an illicit session of sex look like a great way to go.

With rage as well as with fear, the hormones, cortisol and adrenaline overflow the brain. Muscles tense up, heart and breathing rates increase, and we're ready to attack – fast! The original cause of rage can be suppressed, then directed into dangerous outlets. Have you ever experienced this in a sudden surge of road rage?

The traditionally termed "pleasure" does not begin to describe this level 3 emotion. It's what our remote ancestors felt when tucking into their favorite (raw and bloody!) haunch of wooly mammoth after scouting for food for a week. This emotion is extremely intense.

Nowadays, you feel pleasure when your team wins the baseball game or during a delirious love-making session with a close and intimate partner. Pleasure can also be the high of hitting the jackpot at the casino or an injection of speed. Serotonin and dopamine flood the brain synapses. As you saw earlier, our daily quiet joys don't come close.

During recovery, you learn to warm your heart with what author Barbara Kingsolver calls "small wonders." Examples are the lushness of the first summer plum, the intricate spiral of a sea-shell, your first glimpse of sea waves after being landlocked for months.

Later in human evolution, the rational brain, the cortex, developed. It's equivalent to the Adult Part, lucid and coherent, enabling you to see things clearly and problem-solve. As you practice the tools in this book, the Adult Part will learn to control Level 3's negative emotions.

The Brain and Negative Emotions

Rick Hanson and Richard Mendius, authors of *Buddha's Brain*, explain that in primordial times, anxious vigilance was necessary for survival – "The ones that lived to pass on their genes paid a *lot* of attention to negative experiences." We constantly kept watch for the next saber-toothed tiger on the prowl. The brain's negative bias remains part of our physical makeup to this day, contributing heavily to addictions.

The good news is that we can change the brain's bias from negative to positive. Consider this scenario: You and Patrick have chosen the wedding ring. The wedding date has been set. Then he runs off with your best friend. A double whammy. You've been deceived by both of them. Churning thoughts don't let you sleep. "How could they do this?" "I trusted him, I trusted her." "I've already bought my dress, now I'll have to return it." "I should have seen it coming." "No wonder he likes her better than me. I'm fat, freckled, and my ears are too big."

You're caught in a tortured whirlwind of emotion. Rage, humiliation, panic, betrayal, heartache, terror, self-hatred, despair. You seriously consider Hamlet's advice to Ophelia. Maybe you *should* get yourself to a nunnery. Or jump off Brooklyn Bridge. Or better still, take in a session of cybersex then catch some weed.

When you recover and return from Neolithic thoughts of revenge, the Adult rational brain and the Good Parent take over. You turn your attention to the positive. Patrick hates dogs. Now you can buy that wonderful standard poodle from the animal shelter. You and the poodle can lead Sierra Club canine hiking trips. You don't have to watch any more of Patrick's boring macho football games. You'll cut your hair. You have to please him no longer. He's kinda short and paunchy anyway. Patrick likes hip-hop. Now you can buy a whole season's worth of symphony tickets. How about checking out the Meditation Meetup Group? And painting the bathroom purple might be fun.

Hanson and Mendius claim that thoughtful, constant and deliberate switching from the negative to the positive makes lasting brain changes.

Emotions and the Body

Have you noticed that emotions are expressed through the body? Many of our verbal expressions link body and emotions: "I felt it in my bones," "He's a pain in the neck," "I was so excited my heart was racing." We talk about "heartache" and "gut feeling." Emotions can be so intense or so inhibited they are not even felt. They are seldom acknowledged and processed.

That's why only "talk" therapy can fail to cure the addiction. It ignores the body. When you are aware of your body and develop a rapport with it, you have taken an important step in combating your harmful habit.

The challenge is to bring emotions to awareness and experience them. Anesthetizing them with a trip to an erotic movie, your favorite hash dealer, or to Stonehenge Mall for that emerald silk shirt you'll never wear, won't do the trick. For a lasting cure, *feel* your emotions – the tight shoulders, the lump in your throat. Use your rational brain to process them.

Here are some methods to deal with your emotions:

- Spot the red flag.
- Scan your emotional traffic.
- Pinpoint the emotion.
- Identify the trigger.
- Express the emotion.

Spot the Red Flag

An overwhelming urge to plunge into your addiction is your first indication that a powerful emotion is flooding you. Now – and this is the hardest part – stop that impulse even if it's only for a few seconds. Observe the 3-second rule, a 3-second pause to distract yourself. Take a few deep breaths all the way from your stomach and relax your shoulders and mouth.

Find something you can see or hear – the willow outside the window, the drone of a plane, your neighbor chatting to his dog. You may have to do this over and over until you're in control again. Now brainstorm 10 positive things in your life.

Bill Herring of Atlanta Counseling, Therapy and Coaching for Healing and Growth writes: "Consider a match dropped in a dry forest: initially the fire is small and can easily be extinguished. But a person who doesn't pay attention or who delays taking action soon discovers that even a small flame can quickly spread out of control with devastating repercussions." Cravings and negative emotions need discharging before they overwhelm you.

Scan Your Emotional Traffic

A clenched stomach, tight jaw, or hunched shoulders are body signals. A sinking feeling in your stomach is depression. A knot in your stomach is apprehension or fear. Tight shoulders mean anxiety. If your head is bursting, you're frustrated or overwhelmed by worrisome thoughts. Is your Mad Monkey Mind acting up again? A racing heart translates as fear or excitement. Is your diaphragm clamped down with suppressed anger? Are you experiencing a general feeling of gloom and loneliness that has its roots in the past? Ask yourself what your anxiety might be hiding or your depression pushing down. Get a handle on what you're feeling. Connect it with your Challenging Parts.

Pinpoint the Emotion

Bland, overused terms or clichés can prevent the expression of emotions. Because emotions vary in duration and intensity, it's helpful to have alternatives to name them. For example, if you're nervous, try to define more precisely what you're feeling. Are you apprehensive because you're planning to return Walt's engagement ring? Perhaps you're concerned about hurting his feelings. Or are you escalating into terror? That the relationship with Walt is good as it gets and you'll never find anyone better?

Here are some alternatives for our usual emotions:

Anxious: Nervous, concerned, worried, restless, fretful, apprehensive, uneasy

Depressed: Miserable, dejected, low, glum, down, despondent, disheartened

Angry: Annoyed, fuming, irritated, mad, livid, heated, irate, raging, frustrated, gnashing teeth, incensed, furious

Joyful: Blissful, fantastic, pleasant, carefree, pleasurable, wonderful, happy, elated, feeling up

Loving: Adoring, worshiping, be devoted to, be fond of, like, caring for, feeling affection for, passionate, romantic

Lonely: Forlorn, lost, abandoned, deserted, friendless, isolated, solitary, secluded, cut off, remote, detached, alienated

Painful: Aching, heartache, stinging, sore, a twinge, smarting, agonized

Fearful: Scared, frightened, terrified, petrified, timid, afraid, guarded, paralyzed, insecure

Grieving: Unhappy, sad, desperate, weepy, despondent, heartbroken, distressed

Identify the Trigger

Alcoholics Anonymous use the acronym HALT: Hungry, Angry, Lonely, Tired. This helps people identify the triggers that make them want to reach for a drink. Other triggers can be sad, anxious, scared, cold, hot, or overwhelmed. A memory of a former situation in which you felt frustrated or helpless may be haunting you. If you struggle with Basic Badness, even a success might cause an addiction attack.

Which triggers kick off your cravings? They could be sparked by certain people, objects, events, or particular times of day that you connect with your addiction. Triggers may be places such as bars, fast food joints, clothes outlets, massage parlors, the house where you first tried heroin, a casino ad on a billboard. Or the smell of cigarette smoke, pot, or coffee.

Were you in a high-risk situation? Or set off by a harsh word from your spouse, no word from your sister for ten days, a frown on your supervisor's face, an argument with your teen? Illness or physical pain can activate the abandoned Child inside you. Jacob would dive into an Internet craps game each time he came home from his dysfunctional family's Thanksgiving dinner. Eventually he politely declined his family's invitation and celebrated Thanksgiving with a group of friends.

Express the Emotion

In the past, negative influences suppressed your feelings. Now is the time to voice them. Then they'll cease taking refuge in the addiction. Journaling and drawing are effective. Buy yourself a notebook. Journal in it each day. Express both your positive and negative emotions. Drawing your feelings with your non-dominant hand allows your inner Children to communicate with you.

Any physical exercise takes you out of your head and into your body. Do you like to walk, run, bike, swim, stretch, dance, take aerobic or yoga classes? Try having a shower. Imagine washing off the feelings. Yell and pound a pillow to release anger. Imagine the emotion as a black cloud in your head. Take a deep breath and blow it away.

You need people with whom you feel safe and understood. These could be trusted friends, partners, or siblings. Share your feelings with them, even if it's hard at first. Groups can be healing and supportive. End the isolation. Loneliness is a large part of the addictive process. The group doesn't need to be centered around addictions. It could be storytelling group, dream group, or creative writing or art program.

A class that fires your interest. Perhaps it's necessary to talk with a professional. Resources are at the end of this book.

Connecting with your emotions is a big step towards integrating the puzzle pieces of yourself. Stephanie Austin, a well-known astrologist, says, "Water corresponds with feelings; both must flow. Stagnant water breeds disease, and repressed feelings make us ill."

Kimberly Young, PhD, developed the first empirically-based treatment plan for Internet addiction. She founded the Center for Internet Addiction. Young developed the CBT-IA model for treating Internet addiction.

CBT-IA utilizes a three-phase approach. Firstly, behavior modification is used to gradually decrease the amount of time spent online. Then cognitive therapy refocuses thinking to regain control of Internet use. The third phase applies harm reduction techniques. The population that Long treats varies, from teens to people far older. Denial about this addiction is common. Young receives few self-referrals. Usually a family member calls her.

Internet addiction often starts gradually, using chat rooms with friends and spending time online. Young believes that in the United States, Internet addiction can be more pervasive than alcoholism. Contributing to Internet addiction, are the game manufacturers who publicize enticing games. Withdrawal symptoms are common. Often other addictions such as alcoholism and drugs are involved.

"Sadly," says Young, "Loneliness is a problem I often hear about from people with Internet addiction. Lonely people are more likely to become addicted. They become even more socially isolated. It's a vicious cycle. Even if they spend all their time on social media, they are still physically alone."

Excessive Internet and mobile phone use has damaging effects on relationships. Internet infidelity accounts for a growing number of divorce cases.

HIDDEN HUNGERS

WHAT IS THE EMPTINESS, the hunger you're trying to fill with your harmful habit? In this chapter, we look at your Hidden Hungers; what you are missing in life, and what your very soul hungers for. As we said at the beginning of this book, people with addictions have difficulty in making positive connections in their lives.

In order to identify your Hidden Hungers, we'll explore the following important areas of connection:

- Body
- Family
- Relationships
- Vocation
- Living situation
- Recreation
- Community

Body

To heal from an addiction, it's important to respect and appreciate the biological miracle that's your body. It's a valuable tool that works hard for you. Consider the function of your legs, your hands, back, your digestive system, kidneys, liver, heart, genital, and urinary systems.

Work on changing negative attitudes towards the shape, size, and height of your body. Take care of it with exercise, deep breathing, nourishing foods, rest, sound sleep, and relaxation. Do you ignore your body signals? Observe your body's reactions to addictive behavior. Notice how your body feels after you've been bingeing on candy, pot, or alcohol. Or spending hours hunched over your laptop.

Come home to your body. It's time to oppose your negative body image and let your inner being shine through. No need to purge that self you are, or suppress it by taking in toxic substances. Trust your body's wisdom. Be its supporter, not its foe. Befriend your body – it's the house of your soul.

Family

As we discussed earlier, members of the ADF are disconnected from one another. Growing up in this family distorts reality. It influences our belief system. It sets us up for the Dark Spiral of addiction. Healing from an addiction involves letting go of the past. Now you can enlarge your world beyond the confinement of family conditioning.

If your own family is unsupportive and disconnected, your "family" might be close friends, an organization, or a community. As Harper Lee said in *To Kill a Mockingbird*, "You can choose your friends but you can't choose your family."

Relationships

All relationships have their challenges. Addictions occupy the mind, making it easy to deny and ignore problems. The addictive substance or behavior becomes the primary focus in life. People with addictions go for the quick fix. They get that fix through social networking sites or with other players in a card game. Then they don't have to go through the intimidating process of forming solid and lasting connections.

Assess the different types of relationships in your life. Evaluate your intimate relationships (partner, sibs, or close friends), then other relationships (friendly, work-related, and social). We unconsciously copy the old, destructive patterns of relationship of our family. Do you choose incompatible partners, friends, and workmates who let you down? That affirms your belief in your Basic Badness.

Which relationships feel easy to be in? Which are difficult, boring, tense, or toxic? Which do you need to accept? Which can you let go? Can you put limits on those relationships you don't enjoy? Jenny's mother called her daily, complaining about everything from the high price of eggs to her neighbor's barking dog and her loneliness. Jenny spent some months in therapy, working on her guilt about her mother. She finally gathered up her courage and told her mother that a weekly call was all she would accept. And no complaints!

You have to continue certain relationships because of work or family requirements. Any you need to limit, change, or negotiate? If so, how? And how will you go about finding other relationships that are nurturing, supportive, and have a balance of give and take?

Vocation

What are your interests and passions? It's important to feel excitement and enthusiasm about your vocation, whether you're retired, a homemaker, a student, or go to work each day. Perhaps you have outgrown your career and are disenchanted with it. Think about what you need in a vocation. Certainly the money is important, but not the only factor. Material and spiritual abundance come from the same source.

Sometimes only a change of attitude towards your work is necessary to appease this Hidden Hunger. Other times the change needs to be more drastic, like looking for another position or finding a job that doesn't entail a two-hour commute each way.

Perhaps excessive drinking, drug taking, or going out for a meal is part of the company culture. If the job includes going to bars and clubs after work, frequently entertaining clients with a drink, a smoke, or a rich meal, your addiction will be hard to beat. If you missed out on schooling because of the addiction, it's time to think about further education to achieve job satisfaction.

Living Situation

A certain city or country can feel like home. Only too often we stay in a place because it's familiar or the job is good. These are important considerations, but they can hamper fulfillment. Your home symbolizes and expresses your feelings about yourself. It's important that it welcomes you each time you step through the front door. That it gives you a sense of relaxation, peace, and well-being.

Starhawk, a writer on women and spiritual development, tells of the stork carrying basketfuls of embryos to their destinations. Most of the embryos wait quietly, their little hands folded. But some – and I'd say that includes those of us who develop addictions – are so excited they can't keep still. They jump up and down and fall – into the wrong place! It takes them a good deal of time to make their way back to a satisfying living situation. Milan Kundera says, "A person who longs to leave the place where he lives is unhappy."

Recreation

How do you amuse and entertain yourself? The word "recreation" is "re-creation." Recreate yourself through enjoyable and satisfying pastimes, hobbies, and interests. When you are preoccupied with addictions, it's difficult to consider other kinds of fun. With some work, your pull toward addictive substances or behaviors can be channeled into recreational outlets.

Brainstorm some opportunities for fun and recreation. They are usually found in organizations or groups. A weekly aerobics session, hiking club, French class, or Shakespeare society are healthier than spending time and money in addictive behaviors that do not nourish.

Community and Beyond

It's hard for teens to resist the temptation of alcohol, cigarettes, or drugs. They need to be part of the gang. They try forbidden fruit, rebelling against parents. If this turns into an addiction it becomes isolating. It combats the natural desire for community.

Thin-skinned Highly Sensitive People are often loners. We are prone to feeling rejected. This makes social interaction difficult. As you feel more at home in your communities, look beyond them. Injustices, poverty, war, and issues like the pollution of our planet and global warming could be opportunities for your healing. You may become active in collecting blankets for the homeless, volunteering to clean up a creek, or fundraising for an animal shelter. "As you change yourself, you change the world," says Bobby Sager.

Hopefully you can now gauge your degree of connection with your Hidden Hungers. You can decide what is working for you in each area of your life, and what you need to change.

I offer the following tools to satisfy your Hidden Hungers:

- Ringing in the changes
- Structure and routine
- Great expectations
- Connecting with your dreams

Ringing in the Changes

Filling your inner emptiness involves significant change in your life. To quote Heraclites, "You cannot step into the same river twice." Change is uncomfortable and unsettling – and the only constant. Consciously making changes in the areas of life we discussed can be scary. That's moving beyond your comfort zone into unknown territory. The Israelites, after crossing the Red Sea to freedom, heartily wished they were back in slavery. They complained. "We had all the bread and meat we wanted back then." (Not that I would have believed them – meat was only for aristocrats. And manna tasted much like bread, I hear!)

Change does not have to be drastic in order to break out of old patterns. Try out some new experiences. Start small, just one step at a time until you become comfortable. Start your day with 10 minutes of journal writing. Do some stretches first thing in the morning instead of rushing to your coffee machine. Take a different route to work. Then you won't be tempted by a cravings for a Big Mac or a trip to the pub where so many drinking hours were spent.

Consider changing the way you interact socially. In order to heal, it's vital to seek out friendly communities that support and interest you. These could be religious organizations, neighborhood or therapy groups, interests or causes you believe in.

To ease into this gently, try the old therapist trick – listen, listen, listen! Most people love to talk and love to be listened to.

Start by asking a general question, "How long have you be-
longed to this group?" or "I love that pin you're wearing, where
did you get it?" Follow this up with gentle questions based on
their answers. Before long, people will pour out their souls to
you and consider you a friend.

> When I was 15 years old, smoking cigarettes and pot
> was cool. I wanted to be like my friends. They all smoked.
> I got a lot of pressure from them. They sneaked money
> from their parents, and saved up their allowance. So did I.
> By the time I was 18, I was going through a cigarette pack
> and a few pot sessions each day.
> Then I married. I had always dreamed of having chil-
> dren. My obstetrician warned me of smoking while preg-
> nant. It damages the coming child. That's when I started
> to reduce the smoking. It was easier to give up the pot,
> since I still had my cigarettes. Then I very slowly began to
> cut down on the cigarettes. It wasn't slow enough. I went
> through withdrawal. It ranged from no sleep, to anxiety
> and depression. I'd gently rub my stomach, and feel the
> new life inside me. I'd have my spouse sing lullabies to me
> and my unborn infant.
> I still crave a cigarette, but refuse to give in. I want to
> give my baby a healthy start.

Structure and Routine

Changing your routines is an important part of recovery.
Want to see chaos in action? Look at the ADF. No consistent
routine there! Flying plates, screaming and shouting, tense si-
lences, dour looks erupting at a moment's notice. Structuring
your time gives a sense of stability to offset your past. Fixed
routines give you something to count on. Without your harmful
habit, an evening can feel very long. Without routine as king,
you'll be at the mercy of cravings.

Regular sleep patterns head the list. Any addiction plays
havoc with sleep. Going to bed and getting up at the same time

every day sets your internal clock. It allows for deeper sleep, offering your mind a starting and stopping point each day. Begin and end the day with a series of stretches or yoga poses.

Eating meals of a similar type around the same time every day offers a sense of dependability. That keeps your blood sugar steady. Incorporate regular exercise into your daily routine. It's a way to escape the stresses of the day. It makes you feel really good, too. Perhaps, eventually, as good as a hit of coke, don't you think?

Special times for being around friends, partners, children are part of the structure. Also set times for kicking back, meditation, throwing a frisbee for Buster, taking the kids to the local swimming pool, doing the laundry, preparing a gourmet meal just for you. Or taking in an old-time movie, a play, an art exhibition, or summer-filled strawberries at the farmers' market.

"A place for everything and everything in its place" adds structure to your life. Being late for work because you've mislaid the house key is frustrating. If you start your day on that bad note, ending the day with a binge is appealing. Knowing that your keys are hanging in the hall closet, reading glasses are next to the bed, and the tomatoes can be found in the vegetable bin adds security.

The common theme is consistency. Routines and structure give the safety and reliability you need.

Great Expectations

Do you expect too much or too little from yourself, others, and from life? The beginning of a relationship, whether with partners, communities, friends, or a new work situation can seem wonderful. This is the Honeymoon Stage. We fully expect it to remain that way. At last, after lots of digging, we've reached the treasure chest!

Then things turn bad. You notice the dark side of the moon. Mr. or Ms. Wonderful are not perfect after all. He leaves his clothes on the floor. She uses your toothpaste. Your workmate Priscilla ignores you at the office party. You dislike your new supervisor. The world has let you down. Again. You withdraw from the situation without dealing with it. You brood over the situation with a Bacardi rum or rebound into the arms of the next lover.

Because the ADF is unpredictable, you might have felt cared for in certain situations, and abandoned in others. This produces black and white thinking – that people and situations are either good or bad. It parallels addiction issues. You believe you're a good person because you're abstinent. Or you're worthless because you've succumbed to lure of a hooker or a snort of smack.

Life consists of a mixture of good and bad, despair and joy, things that work and those that don't. It's like the black and white of the Yin Yang symbol representing the ancient Chinese understanding of polarities. The outer circle represents the whole. The black and white shapes within the circle represent the interaction of two energies. They are the "yin" (black) and "yang" (white). Let go of black and white thinking. Just accept the good with the bad, the ups and the downs, without stress. The less stress in your life, the less you'll be drawn to your harmful habit.

Connecting With Your Dreams

What would make your life more interesting, exciting, worthwhile, meaningful? What have you always wanted to do, but never got around to? What might put flavor and color into your life? Joseph Campbell gave this good advice, "Follow your bliss." How about going back to school to study linguistics, trying a different relationship, a yoga class, hang gliding lessons, or planning a trip to China? Or simply going to a different market for your groceries.

Past conditioning makes us question the validity of our Hidden Hungers. "Are they real or am I just being fanciful and self-indulgent?" Look at what you can change and what you need to accept. That beats spiraling into depression then dropping down into the addictive pattern.

Here are some helpful hints:

- Throw away the "shoulds" and "oughts."
- Accept the legitimacy of your wants, needs, and desires.
- Decide on five things you love to do and prioritize them.
- Bring in your Natural Children to show you how to be creative, expressive, playful, and spontaneous.
- Try some things you loved to do as a child.
- Channel your self-expression into creative outlets.

Ginny Rutledge Mosby, MA, MFT, is the manager of the Sexual Recovery Program at the Community Presbyterian Counseling Center in Danville, CA. Mosby trained in CSAT – a task-oriented approach to sexual addiction – with the International Institute for Trauma and Addiction Professionals (IITAP).

The institute was founded by Patrick Carnes who states, "People addicted to sex come from rigid, inflexible families where there can be a 90% chance of sexual, physical, or emotional abuse." Carnes brought sex addiction to public and professional awareness.

Mosby says, "Sex addiction is more hidden and underground than other types of addiction. There is a great deal of shame attached to it. When the husband is sexually addictive, the wife's trauma is similar to a rape trauma. In these cases, the harm reduction model is not an option. The addiction has to be terminated."

Mosby sees an increase of sexual addiction with the Internet's readily available pornographic sites. Men who have never been addicted in this way often turn to the Internet after retirement.

{ 14 }

YOUR INNER CORE SELF

NOW WE EXPLORE a deeper level of healing – connecting with your Inner Core Self. The core of the body is between the navel and the breastbone. It's physically strengthened in workouts, yoga, and the martial arts. Similarly, it's important to build up your spiritual and emotional Inner Core Self to combat an addiction.

"Know thyself" is an ancient Greek saying. Knowing yourself means respecting your needs and desires. Your self-confidence and self-esteem have everything to do with an ability to be guided from within. This means following your inner guidance, your *internal* locus (location) of control. An addiction is caused by obedience to the *external* locus of control – that mixture of upbringing, circumstances, and societal pressure. Do you automatically obey the wishes of others? Nicholas Christopher says, "Never be distracted from your own true course. You won't find it on somebody else's map."

Do you sometimes feel a certain course of action is just right for you? It's important to consider these inner promptings. (The trick here is to distinguish your inner promptings from your Conditioned Child's or Critical Parent's intrusive demands.)

When you're operating from your Inner Core Self, you're aware of your behavior and its impact on others. Because of the connection between yourself and the world, harming yourself hurts your family, friends, children, community. Cigarette and pot smoke and destructive Internet interactions harm others and our environment. Those who live from their authentic sense of self constantly strive to live consciously. They actively make choices that are nourishing and beneficial to themselves and others.

> My father was a baseball fan. He pushed me hard. At 16 years old, I was already starring in a major team. My goal in life was to be a second Babe Ruth. Baseball was my life, my identity. It was a source of immense pride for my parents. Then, during a fast game, I slipped and fell. I broke my hip. It never healed completely. I was left with a limp and constant pain. I could play no longer. I felt lost, confused about who I was.
>
> Vicodin was freely prescribed by my busy doctor. "After all," I thought, "Prescription medication is safer than street drugs." It was not long before I was addicted. I found an online supply: "Buy pain medication without prescription." Then my grades began to slip. I lost friends, and could not get a date. That's when I entered therapy. When I turned 18, I left home and went to India. Inspired by Mother Teresa's work, I raised funds and started a school for street children and education for their parents. That mission in life made me whole again. I created a new identity and a new self.

These guidelines will help you manifest your Inner Core Self:
* Self-actualization
* The virtue of selfishness
* Boundaries
* Letting go
* Awareness
* Detachment

Self-actualization

Are you at the mercy of other's whims? Or do you determine your own fate? Do you see yourself as growing, learning? Expanding your ideas and your life? Abraham Maslow developed a humanistic view of personality. He proposed a theory of self-actualization and motivation based on the study of healthy and creative people. He defined self-actualization as "the desire to fulfill our potential." Maslow viewed autonomy as a mark of self-actualization.

Qing Xia and her husband, Bao, were married for 40 years. When he died of a stroke, Qing Xia felt lost and disoriented. The couple had spent many peaceful hours working together in their yard. They'd planted arbors, a rose garden, a vegetable bed, pear, plum, orange, and apple trees. Each room was like a shrine to Bao. Everything in her house reminded her of him. The silence of the empty house made her ache.

Qing Xia realized that the yard demanded a lot of upkeep. Her best friend, also from Hong Kong and neighbors of her age, had left the area. Young families intensely involved with their children's lives moved in. Food, especially chocolate, became a major source of comfort for her. It resulted in a substantial weight gain, diabetes, and heart palpitations. Her doctor warned her of the possibility of a heart attack.

She finally took the courageous step of selling her house, downsizing to a condominium in an active senior village. She enjoyed her new neighbors who stopped to chat at every opportunity. In the ceramics studio, she discovered her gift for sculpture.

She also made a host of Chinese-speaking companions. Qing Xia invited her neighbors over for a house-warming party, gave away her stash of chocolate, and started to develop friendships.

Autonomous people are creative and self-directed. They control their own destiny. Self-development and inner growth are priorities for the self-actualized person.

The Virtue of Selfishness

Were you ever called "selfish" by a parent or partner? "Self-ish" and "self-centered" have a bad rap. "Self-centered" could translate as knowing what's right for you. Do you feel centered in the truth of who you are? When you've manifested your Inner Core Self, you feel fulfilled and prosperous. Only then do you have enough to give others.

Being codependent, allowing others to behave irresponsibly or negatively around you, produces feelings of helplessness and frustration. Then you're tempted to fall back into your tussles with a harmful habit.

Here are some tips for centering yourself in your truth:

- Put limits to what you are willing to do for others.
- Allow others to have their own emotional stuff.
- Avoid feeling responsible for others' feelings or behavior.
- Assert your deservedness in reaching for what you want .
- Please yourself.
- Decide for yourself what feels right for you.
- Find relationships with those with whom you feel safe and comfortable .
- Look at what you can realistically expect from others.
- Tell yourself it's OK to:
    - Make a mistake, not be perfect (or thin!)
    - Succeed (or fail!)
    - Ask for help (or directions)
    - Say NO (nicely)
    - Cry, be confused, angry, or sad

Boundaries

Setting boundaries is essential for those of us in recovery. In the dysfunctional home of the ADF, boundaries were too rigid, leading to suppressed emotions and distant relationships. Or they were enmeshed, depriving children of personal identity. Healthy boundaries let you decide what and what not you'll accept. What consequences might you give if someone violates your boundary? You could say, "If you continue to put me down, I can't be around you."

At age 20, Peter Blake was delighted to escape his small, sleepy town in Oregon. He'd won a scholarship to study medicine at Harvard. His proud parents predicted a dazzling future. But after a few months he became obsessed with *Monsters of Planet 44A.* This was an Internet universe of knights and ogres, wizards and orcs. It brought images of rival armies struggling for power, mysterious treasures, endless possibilities.

Peter began to skip classes. Text messages from Etu, his best friend in Oregon, went unnoticed. Emails from parents and teachers were ignored. Peter had abandoned himself for an engrossing, virtual world. There he was a mighty conqueror, striding alien stars. In real life he'd become a failure and recluse.

His fingers paused over the computer keys when he heard knocking on the door.

Dazed from playing his Internet game for 38 hours straight, he sank into a soiled armchair. He hadn't left his apartment for 10 days, had not showered or shaved. Empty pizza cartons littered the floor. The knocking turned to hammering. He staggered to the door.

Fresh from the airport, Etu took in the scene before him with horror. "My reality had become *Planet 44a*," Peter confessed to his counselor at Three Oaks Inpatient Center. His parents sent him there after a frantic phone call from Etu. The stint at Three Oaks took four months. Peter had to redo his year at Harvard. When he graduated with honors, Etu was at the ceremony, cheering him on.

People with healthy boundaries share their thoughts and feelings. They take care of their own needs. They can say "no" when necessary. And bear in mind what Paul Coelho said, "When you are saying 'yes' to others, make sure you are not say 'no' to yourself."

Thin-skinned Highly Sensitive People need extra self-protection. It's treason to your Inner Core Self to let others step over your line in the sand.

Letting Go

The Second Noble Truth of Buddhism states that the cause of suffering is craving or *tanha*. By craving what we cannot have, for instance, that stubborn desire to light up our fourth Lucky Strike, we double our suffering. When we clutch onto our addictions, we increase our difficulties. We torture ourselves with self-blame, self-disgust, anger, depression, and anxiety. The solution is to let the craving go. We'll explore methods for doing this later on in the book.

"The greatest meditation is a mind that lets go," said Atisha, an 11th century Tibetan Buddhist master.

Awareness

Are you aware of the turning leaves in autumn or the glum expression on your neighbor's face? That your new pot plant, a costly Ficus Benjamina, is dry and wilting? Are you conscious of being hungry, thirsty, tired, bored, frustrated? Are you aware that coffee (and the people!) at the Kind Friends committee meeting make you dizzy and nauseous? Awareness is focusing, paying attention. It's the opposite of dissociation. Certainly, living in the throes of addiction is the very negation of awareness. Being aware of your body and senses brings you back from negative thoughts. Awareness helps you detach from cravings.

The following practice will increase your awareness. It can be done wherever you are – sitting on your couch in the living room, lying on grass, or even washing the dishes:

- Feel your feet on the floor, your back against the chair, your hands on your lap, and the texture of clothes against your skin.
- Pay attention to your posture.
- Where are your feet are in relation to your torso?
- Are you tense? Where in your body?
- Release the tension with a deep breath.
- Sniff the air. What can you smell?
- Gaze through the nearest window. What can you see?
- How does your body feel after hours at the computer or an ear bent to your smart phone?

At your next meal, focus on the sensation of taste. Note differences of size and textures of various foods. Are you plagued by busy thoughts? Obsessing about the next drink, troubled by sexual fantasies, or dreading the next lonely Saturday night? Awareness of your thoughts, emotions, and energy level can prevent addictive behavior.

Here are some helpful tips:

- Focus on your present emotional state.
- Notice your energy level.
- Does your energy increase or decrease with a certain thought? (This is also a good yardstick to measure whether something or someone is right for you.)
- Is that thought useful or not? If not, visualize it drifting away, an autumn leaf dropping from the tree.
- The acronym ACE – Accept, Change, or Eliminate – gives options for situations in which you feel trapped or overwhelmed.

Detachment

Can you disentangle yourself from Level 3 emotions when your buttons are pushed? Detachment halts that knee-jerk impulse to reach for a third caramel cookie or a second martini. Detachment is not disconnecting from others. Seeing situations dispassionately instead of becoming emotionally overwhelmed leads to self-empowerment and good relationships. It facilitates coming to grips with difficult circumstances.

Here are some techniques to detach from upsetting people or circumstances:

- Emotionally step back from difficult or overwhelming situations.
- Let thoughts come and go without reacting.
- Imagine you're watching that situation on TV.
- Play detective or therapist. If your friend Janice loses it each time you mention your new date, work out why it upsets her. You could then respond with compassion, rather than irritation.
- Are you judging situations or other people? This is a version of negative thinking. As we said, negative thoughts can spiral you into addictive behavior.
- Let your inner Adult do some problem-solving. How could you resolve this situation? Avoid a similar one in the future?

Your gifts and talents were ignored and suppressed. You could not be your authentic self or fulfill your potential. Turning to an addiction was the result. That was in the past. As Doctor Seuss, author and illustrator said, "Be who you are and say what you feel, because those who mind don't matter and those who matter don't mind."

It's not too late to manifest your Inner Core Self and fill your life with joy and prosperity. *Tempus fugit.* Time flies. *Carpe diem.* Seize the day!

Holly Holmes-Meredith, MA, MFT, is a Master Reiki teacher and certified clinical hypnotherapist. She is the director of the HCH Institute for Hypnotherapy and Psycho-Spiritual Trainings. The institute offers comprehensive studies and certifications in hypnotherapy, energy therapy, shamanic practices, and transpersonal and parapsychological studies. She was influenced by P.M.H. Atwater's *Runes of the Goddess* which proposes the voice of the spirit over the voice of the ego.

Holmes-Meredith's passionate interest in the psychospiritual is based on opening up all dimensions of experience. She utilizes regression therapy to discover earlier experiences in past lives that cause negative conditions in this life. Methods used to straighten out the energy system are hypnotherapy and the holistic modes mentioned above.

Holmes-Meredith treats many addictions and has been particularly successful in helping people quit smoking. "The prime directive of the work," she says, "is to engage the Higher Self. Addictions are caused by a spiritual or energetic disruption. There is a need to look beyond the addiction."

THE SATISFIED SOUL

THE SATISFIED SOUL is your center of inner wisdom, your sense of purpose and meaning, empowerment, and fulfillment. Satisfy your soul with your dedication (but not obsession!) to parenthood, running marathons, growing heirloom tomatoes, flipping breakfast pancakes for the homeless, working toward world peace, greening the environment. You might find soul-satisfaction in a belief in your country, religion, a political stance, or your principles of racial, class, or sexual equality.

Your Satisfied Soul is both within and outside you, transcendent. It's beyond the physical universe, larger than yourself. Have you ever experienced an inner knowing, a feeling that something or someone is just right for you? This comes from your Satisfied Soul. For some, being in nature or in a special room in their home offers peace, comfort, and stimulation. Others find it at the beach or hiking up a steep mountain trail in the Rockies. Some people experience their Satisfied Soul as a belief in a prophet, guru, or higher power: God, the Divine, Adonai, El Shaddai, Christ, Goddess, Shechina, Buddha, Kwan Yin, Source of Life. Do you experience your Satisfied Soul when marveling at a luminous full moon on a still night or at the plump perfection of a baby?

Connection to your inner wisdom, whatever form it takes, provides an inner sense of security. It offers consistency, continuity, an ability to stand up to the stresses and tugs of modern life. This connection gives you the endurance to offset changing life events. Power, passion, and an incentive to release addictive patterns will be yours. The Satisfied Soul is T.S. Eliot's "Still point of the turning wheel."

Learning to connect with your Satisfied Soul involves:

- Breath work
- Working with chakras
- Solitude and silence
- Mindfulness and the Now
- Balance and centering
- Confronting emptiness

Breath Work

Gauge your breathing. Is it shallow or deep? Breathing was our first action on entering this world, our last when leaving it. "Prana" is a Sanskrit word meaning "breath" and also "life-force." In Latin, it's "animus." "Ruach," the Hebrew word for breath, also means "spirit of God." Notice the times when you're anxious and overtaken by obsessive thoughts. Are you feeling an urge to tumble into your harmful habit? That's when you breathe shallowly or hold your breath. You're disconnected from your body, Inner Core Self, and your Satisfied Soul.

Deep breathing all the way from the abdomen floods your body with serotonin, that feel-good neurotransmitter. Use the following breathing techniques to purify toxins and connect with yourself and the world once more.

Basic Breath

1. Close your eyes.
2. Sit or stand comfortably.
3. Breathe in from your belly, letting it gently expand.
4. Feel the air rising into your lungs, chest, throat, and nostrils.
5. Hold the breath for a micro-second, then release it all the way through your body until your stomach compresses.
6. Relax your eyelids as you exhale.
7. The exhalation is longer than the inhalation.
8. Repeat.
9. Do this again, relaxing your mouth.
10. Let a little puff of air out your mouth.
11. Repeat.
12. Relax your shoulders. (These three areas – eyes, mouth, and shoulders – hold the most tension.)
13. Repeat.
14. Now repeat the breathing and relaxation of these areas twice more.
15. Take another breath. As you exhale, breathe out all the tension in your body.
16. Most likely it won't be long before your thoughts drift away from the breath work. As soon as you notice this, gently bring yourself back to your focus on breathing.
17. Open your eyes and sit quietly for a moment. Notice the energy in your body and the absence of tension.

Instant Breath Fix

This is a variation of the Basic Breath, done briefly and with eyes open. You can do it wherever you are. Use the Breath Fix every hour if you're stressed.

1. Inhale and exhale, slowly, deeply, and gently.
2. Inhale once more, then exhale, relaxing your eyes.
3. Repeat.
4. Inhale again, relaxing your mouth as you exhale.

5. Repeat.
6. Inhale, then exhale relaxing your shoulders.
7. Repeat.

Caution

If your breathing is normally shallow, the breath exercises may make you a little dizzy. Support yourself with the back of a chair while doing them.

Working with Chakras

What are chakras?

All living things need a steady supply of energy. Chakras are subtle power centers connecting us to our life energy. A physician or acupuncturist might define chakras as nerve plexuses – systems of connected nerve fibers that link spinal nerves with specific areas of the body. The word "chakra" is derived from the Sanskrit word for "wheel." The chakra system is a column of seven rotating wheels or circles from the base of the spine to the top of the head. In some traditions chakras are visualized as lotuses. Chakra energy is blocked or scattered when we engage in our harmful habits.

Each chakra is a meeting place for the body, mind, emotions, and spirit. Each chakra corresponds to an emotion, an area of the body's anatomy, an acupuncture point, a color, and to one or more of Erikson's stages of life. When a chakra is blocked, the flow of energy is trapped. Then we develop physical or emotional illnesses and are prone to addictions. Working with chakras is a powerful healing tool for you.

This description of chakras and how to work with them brings together many of the previous ideas in this book.

We begin with a chart showing each chakra's characteristics:

Chakra 1: **Root or Base Chakra**

Location: Base of the spine

Central Issues: Survival, safety, self-preservation, foundation, trust

Focus: The body, physical reality, nourishment from the mother

Challenges: Mistrust of oneself, others, and the world, terror of abandonment, dissociation, fear, lack of mothering

Goals: Grounding, being supported by self and others, ability to take care of oneself emotionally and physically, hope and optimism

Developmental stage: Womb to 12 months.

Erikson: Infancy – basic trust or mistrust.

Chakra 2: **Sacral Chakra**

Location: Lower abdomen

Central Issues: Sexuality, sensuality, creativity, self-gratification, exploration

Focus: Emotions, pleasure, creativity

Challenges: Sexual problems, stuck or unexpressed emotions, guilt, lack of creativity, rejection of femininity or masculinity, oversensitivity

Goals: Healthy pleasure, ability to express emotions and needs

Developmental stage: six months to two years

Erikson: Early childhood – autonomy or shame and doubt

Chakra 3: **Solar Plexus Chakra**

Location: Below the diaphragm

Central Issues: Power, self-esteem, energy

Focus: Self-definition, willpower, determination

Challenges: Anger, helplessness, anxiety, sense of worthlessness, victim mentality, grandiosity, narcissistic, power-hungry

Goals: Sense of identity and purpose, self-empowerment
Developmental stage: eighteen months to five years
Erikson: Play Age – initiative or guilt

Chakra 4: Heart Chakra

Location: Chest, heart
Central Issues: Self-love, and love of others, balance, compassion, intimacy
Focus: Relationship, social identity
Challenges: Depression, loneliness, withdrawal, grief, loss of love, despair, lack of empathy
Goals: Giving and receiving love, joy, gratification
Developmental stage: six to eleven years
Erikson: School age – industry or inferiority

Chakra 5: Throat Chakra

Location: Base of the throat
Central Issues: Communication, speaking one's truth, creative and symbolic thinking, listening
Focus: Self-expression
Challenges: Unhealthy communication, manipulation, lying, difficulty with self-expression and creativity, verbosity
Goals: Clear and effective communication, finding one's voice, self-assertion
Developmental stage: six to eleven years
Erikson: School age – industry or inferiority

Chakra 6: Third Eye Chakra

Location: Center of the forehead, brow, between the eyes
Central Issues: Intuition, self-reflection, use of mind and intellect
Focus: Insight, vision

Challenges: Muddled, rigid, or scattered thinking, feeling overwhelmed, literal and concrete perceptions, blocked intuitive faculties, denial, illusion

Goals: Psychic perception, imagination, clear seeing, flexible thinking

Developmental stage: Adolescence

Erikson: Adolescence – identity or role confusion
Young adulthood – intimacy or isolation

Chakra 7: Crown Chakra

Location: Crown of the skull, top of the head

Central Issues: Expanded awareness, search for meaning, grace, spiritual awakening, oneness with the universe

Focus: Connection to the transcendent and the divine

Challenges: Over-intellectualization, cynicism, confusion, dissociation, lack of purpose and meaning, ungrounded spirituality

Goals: Spiritual connection, consciousness, trust in an inner wisdom

Developmental stage: Throughout life

Erikson: Young adulthood – intimacy or isolation
Middle adulthood – generativity or stagnation
Maturity – ego integrity or despair

The Second Spring corresponds to the upper three chakras.

One or more chakras may be dysfunctional – blocked, weak, dominant, scattered, or blown out. This can be due to birth complications, childhood trauma, severe illness, abandonment, insecurity, sexual abuse, or catastrophic life occurrences. Energy and vitality cannot flow freely. You're prone to negative behavior patterns.

For those with addictions, one or more chakras are out of balance, over or under active, or carry a toxin build-up.

The lower three chakras are involved with physical processes and the interaction between the self and the world. The upper three correspond to higher mental and spiritual processes. The heart chakra connects the lower and upper chakras.

The first chakra, the root or base, is your foundation. It grounds and anchors you to your body. It is your bond with the earth, our original Mother, and the physical reality of the Now. The first chakra forms the basis for all the other chakras.

Did you lack a nourishing experience of mothering? As we saw in the section on the family, this is usually true for those struggling with harmful habits. A blocked first chakra causes deeper and more resistant life problems and severe addictions. This happens when basic physical and emotional requirements in life were not met. So we fly into the upper three chakras. We escape the distress embodied in the lower chakras. We're distracted from our rootlessness (first chakra), emotional pain (second chakra), and self-hatred (third chakra). The heart chakra suffers damage in this process. We have difficulty giving and receiving love.

Our life-task is to mother ourselves in all the ways we discuss in this book. We learn how to be our own mothers. We take care of our well-being like a loving mother with her precious child.

Some authorities claim that certain addictions relate to each chakra. A food addiction is an attempt to ground and root us. Food comes from the earth. Marijuana, alcohol, and promiscuity release inhibitions from the second chakra. This enables social ease and relaxation. Caffeine, sugar, nicotine, the rush of gambling, an Internet game, a sex orgy, or a spending spree restore the lost energy of the third chakra. Hard liquor and the hard drugs create the sense of closeness, mind-altering effects, and euphoria, which relate to the heart and three upper chakras.

> I have overcome eating disorders, IV cocaine addiction, nicotine addiction, and unhealthy sexual relationships. As a child, I struggled with loneliness, rejection, shyness, and confusion. I was introspective, had a preoccupation with beauty, and craved excitement. I had a rich fantasy life.
>
> A pattern of painful losses began. My childhood was punctuated by the divorce of my parents at age 2. My father's suicide followed shortly after that. My stepfather was emotionally distant from me.
>
> Beginning at age 12, I sought fulfillment through a string of sexually saturated relationships. I smoked cigarettes, used alcohol and drugs. I spent most of my adolescence and young adult years in therapy with poor results. My adolescence was dominated by an eating disorder. I later it traded for a serious cocaine addiction. After three weeks in rehab, I traded the drug addiction for sexual acting out.
>
> Finally I connected with God. I began a period of spiritual growth that completely transformed my life.
>
> Through this and dogged determination, I overcame all my addictions and destructive behaviors. Then I went on to forge a life worth living. Now I help others overcome their addiction issues.

The upside is that those of us struggling with addictions are easily able to connect with the higher mental and moral processes of the upper three chakras. We have a natural affinity with the transcendent and the divine. It would not be a stretch to say that with healing and clearing of the chakras – especially of the lower three chakras and the heart chakra – we can become the inspired and creative teachers, healers, leaders, and prophets that our world needs so much.

Here are exercises to help you overcome lack of grounding in the first chakra and blockages in the other chakras. I suggest you build some of them into your morning routine. Try them right after getting out of bed.

Grounding Meditation

Stand barefoot, looking at a tree, a garden, or the sky. Feet are six inches apart, knees slightly bent and directly under your hips. Shoulders are relaxed. Your head is upright. Relax your arms. Keep your eyes and chin level. Relax your eyes, mouth, and face.

Begin with a deep breath, in and out. Imagine a line of energy all the way up your legs, and through the core of your torso and neck. Then out through the crown of your head. Imagine a root growing from the first chakra at the base of your spine deep into the earth. The root spreads out like the roots of a sturdy oak tree. It anchors you to the earth. Imagine roots extending from the soles of your feet into the ground. Breathe into them. Then breathe in the powerful earth energy rising through the soles of your feet, up your spine, and to the top of your head.

Mountain Visualization

The starting position is the same as the grounding meditation. Picture a mountain. Become aware of its stillness and strong connection with the earth. Feel the heaviness of the mountain, its permanence. Stay with this image for as long as you need to, breathing deeply from your stomach.

Other Grounding Techniques
- Stamp your feet.
- Walk barefoot on sea sand, grass, or a fluffy carpet.
- Paste a picture of a mountain under a favorite chair.
- Roll a tennis ball beneath each of your bare feet.

- Give yourself a foot massage.

Chakra Checking

Go through the chakra chart above. Check out any blockages in each chakra. Where do you feel chronic pain? Which areas of your body are tight and knotted up? Which parts of your body feel relaxed and loose? Relate this to specific chakras. Which emotions bother you? Which chakras hold your challenges? Which chakras are clear and flowing? For instance, if you are intuitive and enjoy using your imagination, your sixth chakra is balanced and strong. Frequent outbursts of anger point to a blockage in your third chakra. Chronic shoulder tension reflects blockages in the heart or throat chakras.

Chakra Cleansing and Healing

Regular chakra cleansing increases your life energy. It cleans, balances, and enlivens vital energy centers.

Take a few breaths, and relax your shoulders. Place your right hand, palm down, over the first (base or root) chakra. Take a deep breath. As you breathe out, move your hand in a clockwise direction for about five seconds. Imagine wiping a circular window free of dirt. Or visualize a flower slowly opening its petals, absorbing the energy of the sun. Go through each chakra, breathing deeply and gently. From the crown chakra, move downwards through each chakra. When you reach the root chakra, take a few more deep breaths.

Imagine all tension, negativity, and cravings flowing out of your body through your fingers and the soles of your feet. End by resting both hands on the crown chakra on top of your head.

Books by Caroline Myss and Anodea Judith provide detailed information on chakras. They are referenced in my bibliography.

Solitude and Silence

Is your life over-scheduled? Frenetic, over-active whether at home, at work, or even on vacation? Is your life crowded with people? In our pedal-to-the-metal society, we focus on "doing" rather than on "being." The capacity to pull away from the world, to be silent, still, and alone is strangely liberating. It's a marked contrast to the noise and visual stimuli that bombard us.

Solitude is not loneliness or alienation. It's a getting-in-touch with yourself. It's experiencing the Satisfied Soul in a deeper way. Instead of feeling depleted and fragmented, solitude and silence helps us feel centered and whole. The words "whole" and "holy" are similar in sound and meaning. In Hebrew, "shalom" means both wholeness and peace. There's a holy sense of peace in just sitting with yourself. It's coming to terms with who you really are and your place in the world.

Schedule a sacred alone time into each busy day. I offer suggestions a little further on for nourishing yourself during those quiet moments.

Paul Tillich, philosopher and theologian, best known for *The Courage to Be*, said, "Loneliness expresses the pain of being alone and solitude expresses the glory of being."

Mindfulness and the Now

Mindfulness, according to the teaching of the Buddha, is a path to wisdom and enlightenment. He saw it as part of day-to-day life. Certainly, some of the latest psychological techniques incorporate mindfulness for achieving peace and calm. Mindfulness lowers the levels of the stress hormone, cortisol. The body's natural healing system can then operate effectively. It can clean itself of chemical and emotional toxins. Mindfulness regulates fluctuating moods, enhances our immune system, and increases energy.

When we're entangled with the Dark Spiral and its bosom buddy, our harmful habits, we're unaware of the world around us. Mindfulness is useful in controlling unruly and obsessive thoughts. It's the antidote to *mindlessness* – that conditioned reflex to turn to our ancient addictive patterns without considering consequences.

Watch your thoughts and feelings objectively, without judgment. Just let them go their own way without getting tugged into them. You remember that Marge forgot to pick up milk at the market – again! Tell yourself it's not the end of the world – or the end of your relationship. Note the impulse to pick up your smart phone. Breathe that impulse away.

Be mindful during the most mundane of everyday activities. As you wash your hands, be conscious of the water running over them. Feel the air on your skin when you step outside. Developing the observing mind increases pleasure and joy in what you see, hear, smell, and touch: snow capping the mountain peak, the call of migrating Canadian geese, the sharp tang of pine needles, soft petals of a lily.

Are your moments of savoring the present few and far between? Living in the "Now" is another aspect of mindfulness; becoming deeply conscious of each moment. Eckhart Tolle, spiritual teacher, author of *The Power of Now*, calls awareness of the present moment "The Now." Compulsively dwelling on the past and the future is destructive. You were born with the gift of appreciating the present moment. As a child, all your senses were aware of small marvels: the long thin legs of a spider, a trickle of sea-sand through your fingers, the military flight of a troop of pelicans, the pattering of rain on a tin roof. You were taught to ignore these everyday miracles as you grew up.

Tolle says: "The mind is a superb instrument if used rightly. Used wrongly, it becomes very destructive. It is not so much that you use your mind wrongly – you usually don't use it at all. It uses you. Life is Now. There was never a time when your life was not Now, nor will there ever be." When we abandon the Now, our Mad Monkey Mind chases itself on an addictive speed track to nowhere:

- "Maybe I should keep off pot for just one more day. Or maybe I shouldn't."
- "I thought I could handle that that martini. Now I really need another!"
- "Wow! They have a big end-of-year sale at Grandstand Mall."
- "Perhaps I could slip away, find someone for a one-night stand."
- "What will Aunt Tabitha say when she sees all the weight I've gained since last Thanksgiving?"

Mind chatter leads to disconnection from ourselves and alienation from others. A hectic pace of life and the churning of our thoughts keep us from responding to the gifts of life. French existentialist author, Camus, used the word "anomie." You feel anonymous, a nobody. You don't matter. You hardly exist. Is that feeling familiar? Pull yourself away from mind chatter. Immerse yourself in the experience of your senses. What are you touching, seeing, hearing, smelling, tasting – right now?

Balance and Centering

Finding the middle ground, what Aristotle called the "Golden Mean," keeps us stable and centered in the midst of change. Then addressing the addiction and making the necessary changes for healing are not as threatening.

Use the following techniques to center yourself:

- Quiet your mind by thinking of a sturdy oak tree, a rose garden, a robin hopping on the grass, a favorite uncle.
- Pause in your activities each hour to shrug your shoulders, roll them back and forth, and stretch your neck.
- Stand with your feet six inches apart and your body in a straight line. Close your eyes and gently rock forward and back, then side to side. Feel that sense of relief when you regain your balance. If you're uncertain of your balance, hold onto the back of a chair.
- Take time to pat yourself on the back.
- Imagine that your demanding thoughts about food, drugs, alcohol, or sex are on the rim of a wheel. You are in the still center of the wheel, quiet and at peace with yourself.
- Create a special space for yourself. Do you have a room or chair you can set aside for quiet times? On a small table or desk, arrange some meaningful objects: that glass egg from a trip to Mendocino, a spiral shell, arrangement of dried grasses, crystals, a photograph of a much-loved grandmother.

Confronting Emptiness

Do you sometimes feel hopeless and empty? That's when we descend into the negative states of the Dark Spiral. The addiction is an attempt to survive the emptiness. There is another way of perceiving emptiness. Spiritual teachers view emptiness as a path to enlightenment and spiritual growth, a blessing in disguise. Eastern philosophies like Buddhism and Taoism see emptiness (*Śūnyatā*) as a state of stillness, peace, and inner silence.

Emptiness is described in Genesis, "There was darkness upon the face of the earth before creation." Emptiness comes before any type of creativity: the painter's blank canvas, the sculptor's untouched block of stone, the field plowed and fertilized for the farmer.

Look at your feeling of emptiness as an opportunity to transform an addiction. At first, this is scary. Mark Epstein, author of *Going to Pieces without Falling Apart*, says, "Only when we stop fighting with our own personal emptiness can we begin to appreciate the transformation that is available." Paradoxically, allowing yourself to encounter, experience, and process the emptiness enables a fullness of being.

Meditative, inward-turning, and self-reflective practices are the way to stay with emptiness. There are many paths and several tools to discipline, calm, and focus the mind. They are potent means for nourishing yourself. The heart rate lowers, breathing deepens and slows. The body stops releasing cortisol and adrenaline into the bloodstream. Our happiness hormone, serotonin, increases. We become less susceptible to cravings.

Meditative and self-reflective practices calm down our speeding Western minds. Choose one or more of the following:

- *Vipassana*: This is an ancient practice of insight meditation, originally attributed to Gautama Buddha. At its heart is focusing on the breath to concentrate and clear the mind. The Basic Breath may be used for this.
- *Mantras*: Repeat words, phrases, prayers, or sounds.
- *Visualizing:* Close your eyes and imagine a healing space in nature, such as a beach, lake, or mountain.
- *Moving Meditations: A*s you walk, keep your mind on the swing of your arms, the movement of your feet striking

the path before you, a breeze through your hair, or the call
of sparrows. Various types of yoga, Tai Chi, Qi Gong, and
Kum Nye are examples of moving meditations

- *Focusing:* Watch a candle, a crystal, waves crashing on the
  shore, or willows swaying in the wind.
- *Free Association:* Experiment with journaling, memoir
  writing, or drawing. Try drawing with your non-
  dominant hand.
- *Music:* Some CDs incorporate nature sounds with gentle
  and flowing music.
- *Body or Energy Therapies:* Examples of these are chakra
  clearing, Reiki, therapeutic body work, and somatic therapy.
- *Relaxation Techniques*: Starting from the top of your
  head, relax each part of your body down to your toes. Relaxation exercises can be downloaded from the Internet.
- *Energy Work*: Imagine a narrow band of light all the way
  around your body. Breathe out, sending the light further
  out, so it extends first six inches and then further out
  from your body.
- *Affirmations:* You don't have to believe in what you're affirming! Just put it out into the universe. Choose an affir-
  mation for each week, e.g., "I deserve to be happy." Say it
  many times each day.

Resources for meditative techniques and self-reflective practices are in the bibliography at the end of this book. You can
download videos and audios for these on my website:
www.shoshanakobrin.net .

Connecting with Your Satisfied Soul

Once you've grounded yourself and cleared the chakras, imagine
a shower of white light entering the top of your head. Like a
fountain, it cleanses you, mind, body and spirit. Imagine the
light as the illumination of the stars, the energy of the sun and
moon. Or use any image that has meaning for you.

During a contemplative practice, when your mind is quiet, ask your Satisfied Soul for guidance. Be still and let answers and healing come to you. Trust that you have an inexhaustible fountain of wisdom inside you.

> I'm not sure when I decided to go for recovery. Perhaps it was when I went through withdrawal after a five-day, around-the-clock binge on vodka and heroin. All on my own. Not a soul to help me. I felt I was dying. Cold sweats, hot sweats, unable to eat or drink water. I imagined weird shadows in my room. Before calling the hospital, I thrashed in my bed for more than 60 hours. Was that when my rocky road to recovery began?
>
> Or was it when I fell asleep on a bench at the bus stop? I woke to find a gigantic cop, armed to the teeth with guns and a truncheon shaking me. A gutsy, well-dressed lady walked up and asked if I was homeless. Probably she was a volunteer for a homeless shelter.
>
> I managed to stutter "no" before the cop frisked me for drugs. I was arrested, convicted, and put on probation. Maybe it was then I knew I had to find a different route to enlightenment – like sobriety.
>
> Most likely I will never know exactly when or how my recovery began. Possibly it was at 4 a.m. during a hard winter. A hailstorm was rattling the windowpanes. I felt as though I was under fire in a war zone. Dizzy, and with shaking fingers, I punched in the number of the Crisis Center. A woman answered immediately. She soothed and supported me until I could accept her advice. The next day I ended up calling one of her recommended therapists. His gentle voice calmed me down. An overpowering feeling of support swept over me. Life was a terrible mess, torn apart, fragmented. But now I was no longer alone.

Caution

Many of these techniques are refining processes that release toxins. At first you might be over-reactive, anxious, or depressed. You could have physical problems such as stomach upsets or headaches. There could be an upsurge of addictive urges.

It's important to start slowly. Use these techniques for only a few minutes at first, then gradually build up the time. Consider finding a therapist, a teacher, or taking a class so you have professional guidance.

{ 16 }

RECLAIMING YOURSELF

NOW IS THE TIME, time to return. To return to your true self, to your Satisfied Soul.

Right now is the opportunity to choose between the Dark Spiral of the addiction and your Satisfied Soul. Challenges in life are inevitable, but suffering from an addiction is optional.

Your harmful habits are deeply ingrained. But they were learned. They can be unlearned. As Mark Twain said, "Habit is habit and not to be flung out of the window by anyone, but coaxed downstairs a step at a time." That step could be one day at a time, or on bad days, one hour at a time. You recover by creating a new life in which it's easier not to use.

For many weeks, Les became angry whenever I mentioned his daily use of pot. He told me, "Cutting back goes against the grain. I'll never be able to manage without it!" We're so used to our established coping mechanisms. Ending or even reducing them makes us wonder how we'll handle life. When we move out of our comfort zone, we experience anxiety and depression, changes in sleep or appetite. We find ourselves shifting between mountaintops of hope and valleys of despair.

Habit is not destiny. With time and constant work you can let your harmful habits go. Expect a few detours on the path. Don't be taken off balance by relapses. You may still feel a charge around your previous stamping grounds and the buddies you used to hang out with for a drink or a smoke. Passing a casino, your favorite junk food eatery, a brothel, shopping center, or laptop cafe can trigger cravings. Be patient. The trick is to forgive yourself. Dust yourself off. Continue practicing your new and nourishing habits until they are second nature.

Without the defense of the addiction, you'll be more sensitive. Don't be surprised if you overreact when the world doesn't behave the way it should. Life will continue to hurl curveballs in your direction. We all encounter the loss of a job or relationship, illness, or accident. We all face the inevitability of aging and mortality. Expectations and desires are not always met. Fight old tendencies with awareness, mindfulness, persistence, and determination. Create nourishing habits that feed you mentally, physically, emotionally and spiritually. Eventually staying on track becomes comfortable. If you persevere, you *will* achieve healthier ways to handle life's challenges.

When you manifest your Inner Core Self and Satisfied Soul, you'll find a discord, a dissonance with your harmful habit. The stimulation of a prescription painkiller or a shot of Wild Turkey becomes unnecessary. You find your excitement in helping a new neighbor move in, the increasing strength of your arms as you swim laps, exploring an art museum, learning to play the blues on that piano you've neglected for years, having a heart-to-heart with your partner. Your determination to create other outlets for soul-satisfaction will override the fleeting relief or pleasure your addictive behavior provided.

Addictive substances and behaviors are not magical. They will not fill your soul. The magic is in you, in your capacity to remain at the epicenter of yourself regardless of changing circumstances. You may even find yourself grateful for tough times, seeing them as guideposts for your journey. "The cave you fear to enter holds the treasure that you seek," said Joseph Campbell.

Our village in Kenya was so far inland and so untouched that Mombasa seemed like another country. Mother was pounding the meal. My father, uncle, and brothers were tilling the fields. Aunt Jata was teaching Baako and Dziko to weave hemp for our clothing. A smooth, even day in a smooth, even life.

Until the rebels came. I was rinsing laundry in the river, hidden by the mangrove forest. First the sound of heavy boots and rough voices, a child wailing, then shots and screaming that went on and on. More shots, the stench of burning huts. The silence of death.

I remember nothing more until I woke, folded in cool sheets, Sister Beatrice placidly knitting beside me. I could not speak, hardly eat. It was Ferris, the American doctor who arranged for my emigration to the United States, entry into nursing school, and an internship. I pilfered medication to help me sleep without nightmares and get through the empty days.

That was easy until I turned from the medicine cabinet to find my patient, Jane Ellen Watkins, her arm in a sling from shoulder surgery, watching me. "You told me your name, Abebi, means 'asked for girl child,'" she said. "Remember your name."

Two weeks later, I moved into her in-law unit. She soothed and motivated me with her caring until the nightmares, the anguish, and the need for pain pills went away.

Absolve yourself from the false belief that there's something intrinsically wrong with you. You unconsciously (and creatively) "chose" your addiction to protect yourself from intense emotions you couldn't process or understand at the time. People who develop addictions are unusually strong and creative. It takes a lot of strength to endure a past that was rigidly controlled, neglectful, abusive, or catastrophic. You used the addiction to survive.

Now the addiction limits your emotional and spiritual flowering. It no longer serves you.

To go beyond survival and liberate yourself from the obsessive angst of your harmful habit, you need courage. Bear in mind the words of Winston Churchill, "Success is not final, failure is not fatal: it is the courage to continue that counts." The word "courage" comes from the French "coeur," translated as "heart." Your heart is the meeting place of the upper and lower chakras, of heaven and earth. As you struggle to let go of the familiar, take heart. Keep faith with yourself, stay on your path, and honor your selfhood.

In overcoming your harmful habit, you'll make space to relate positively to the world within and around you. Your being will expand as you discover other interests and passions. You contain within you a multitude of gifts to be unwrapped. Many people in recovery see themselves as "wounded healers." After you heal, sharing your experience can help others repair their hurts.

There's a correlation between how you feel about yourself and how the world responds to you. An ancient quote tells us, "As within, so without." When you connect with your Satisfied Soul, you'll attract whatever you need, whenever you need it. Opportunities you've been searching for in vain will miraculously appear.

The Hebrew word "teshuva" has a myriad of meanings: turn, turn back, turn around, salvation. *Teshuva* is the greatest gift you can give yourself – the ability to return to your true and original self, to your Satisfied Soul. Your true self is a pure mountain spring emerging from your depths. Now is the time to seek healing from brokenness. With dedication and perseverance you will return, return to the unique person you are. Trust that you have an inexhaustible fountain of wisdom within you. Buddhists call this the "clear light" – the ability to see the truth, *your* truth, the truth of yourself.

Now is the time to highlight your heavens with a significant sun.

BIBLIOGRAPHY
AND
RESOURCES

Bibliography

Aron, E. (1996). *The Highly Sensitive Person*. New York: Broadway Books.

Bell, R. (1985). *Holy Anorexia*. Chicago: University of Chicago Press.

Berne, E. (1964). *Games People Play*. New York: Ballantine Books.

Bruche, H. (1987). *The Importance of Overweight*. New York: Harper.

Cameron, J. (1992). *The Artist's Way*. New York: Putnam.
(2007). *The Writing Diet*. New York: Penguin.

Capacchione, L. (1991). *Recovery of Your Inner Child*. New York: Simon & Schuster.

Carnes, P. (1992). *Don't Call It Love: Recovery From Sexual Addiction*. New York: Bantam.
(2005). *Facing the Shadow*. Carefree, AZ: Gentle Path Press.

Carrol, M. (2006). *Awake at Work*. Boston & London: Shambhala.

Cohen, B., Giller, E., & Lynn, W. (Eds). (1991). *Multiple Personality Disorder from the Inside Out*. Lutherville, MD: Sidran Press.

Colvin, R. (2008). *Overcoming Prescription Drug Addiction*. Omaha, NA: Addicus.

Cooper, G. (2007). *Never Smoke Again*. New York: Square One Publishers.

Dorsman, J. (1998). *How to Quit Drugs for Good*. New York: Three Rivers Press.

Denning, P., Little, J., & Glickman, A. (2004). *Over the Influence*. New York: Guilford Press.

Engel, L., & Ferguson, T. (1990). *Imaginary Crimes*. Lincoln, NE: IUniverse.

Erikson, E. (1980). *Identity and the Life Cycle*. New York: Norton.

Friedman, M. (1985). *Toward a Reconceptualization of Guilt. Contemporary Psychoanalysis*, 21(4), 501-507.

Goldberg, N. (1990). *Wild Mind: Living the Writer's Life*. New York: Bantam.

Hanson, R., & Mendius, R. (2009). *Buddha's Brain: The Practical Neuroscience of Happiness, Love, and Wisdom*. Oakland, CA: New Harbinger.

Harris, T. (1970). *I'm OK – You're OK*. London: Pan Books.

Hicks, E., & J. (2006). *The Law of Attraction*. Carlsbad, CA: Hay House.

Horn, S. (1996). *Tongue Fu! How to Deflect, Disarm and Defuse any Verbal Conflict*. New York: St. Martin's Press.

Johnson, N. (2009). *The Multiplicities of Internet Addiction*. Burlington, VT: Ashgate Publishing Company.

Judith, A. (1999). *Wheels of Life: A User's Guide to the Chakra System*. Woodbury, MN: Llewellyn's New Age Series.
(2004). *Eastern Body, Western Mind*. Berkeley & Toronto: Celestial Arts.

Khaleghi, M., & Khaleghi, K. (2011). *The Anatomy of Addiction*. New York: Palgrave, Macmillan.

Kobrin, S. (2011). *The Satisfied Soul GuideBook: Your Path to Fulfillment*. Bloomington, IA: AuthorHouse.
(2012). *The Satisfied Soul: Transforming Your Food and Weight Worries*. Bloomington, IA: AuthorHouse.
(2013). *Love, Anger, Power – and Food! A Guidebook for Women*. North Charleston, NC: Create Space.

Lancelot, M. (2007). *Gripped by Gambling*. Tucson, AZ: Wheatmark.

Lelwica, M. (2010). *The Religion of Thinness*. Carlsbad, CA: Gurze.

Mate, G., & Levin, P. (2010). *In The Realm of Hungry Ghosts: Close Encounters With Addiction.* Berkeley, CA: North Atlantic Books.

Milam, J., & Ketcham, K. (1983). *Under the Influence.* New York: Bantam.

Miles, P. (2006). *Reiki: A Comprehensive Guide.* New York: Jeremy Tarcher/Penguin.

Myss, C. (1966). *Anatomy of the Spirit: The Seven Stages of Power and Healing.* New York: Three Rivers Press.

Nakken, C. (1996). *The Addictive Personality: Understanding the Addictive Process and Compulsive Behavior.* Center City, MN: Hazeldon.

Peele, S. (2004). *7 Tools to Beat Addiction.* New York: New Rivers Press.

Penix, T. (2005). *The Sex Addiction Workbook.* New York: New Harbinger.

Prentiss, C. (2005). *The Alcoholism and Addiction Cure: A Holistic Approach to Total Recovery.* New York: Harper.

Rasmussen, S. (2000). *Addiction Treatment: Theory and Practice.* Thousand Oaks, CA: Sage Publications.

Ross, R. (1982). *Prospering Woman.* Mill Valley, CA: Whatever Publishing.

Roth, G. (2010). *Women, Food and God.* New York: Scribner.

Saradananda, S. (2008). *Chakra Meditation.* London: Watkins.

Schüll, N. D. (2012). *Addiction by Design: Machine Gambling in Las Vegas.* Princeton, NJ: Princeton University Press.

Shulman, T. (2008). *Bought Out and Spent: Recovery from Compulsive Shopping and Spending.* West Conshohocken, PA: Infinity Publishing.

Stein, D. (1955). *Essential Reiki.* New York: Random House.

Tillich, P. (1952). *The Courage to Be.* London & New Haven, CT: Yale University Press.

Tillotson, D. (2013). *Overcoming Caffeine Addiction: How to Stop Using the Most Abused Drug in America.* North Charleston, NC: Create Space.

Tolle, E. (1999). *The Power of Now.* Novato, CA: New World Publishing.

Twerski, A. (1997). *Addictive Thinking.* Center City, MN: Hazeldon.

Washton, A. (1984). *Willpower's Not Enough: Recovering from Addictions of Every Kind.* New York: Harper and Row.

Weiss, J. (1993). *How Psychotherapy Works.* New York: Guilford Press.

Yerkovich, M., & K. (2006). *How We Love.* Colorado Springs, CO: Waterbrook.

Young, K. (1998). *Caught In the Net: How to Recognize the Signs of Internet Addiction.* New York: John Wiley & Sons.

Resources

Cali Estes, MSc., Certified Addiction Professional
www.theaddictionscoach.com cali@theaddictionscoach.com

Cynthia Hoffman, MA, MFT
www.cynthiahoffmanmft.com cynthiahoffmanmft@yahoo.com

Jackie Holmes, M.Ed., MFT
Casa Serena Eating Disorders Program
www.casaserenaedp.com info@casaserenaedp.com

Holly Holmes-Meredith, MA, MFT, Certified Clinical Hypnotherapist.
HCH Institute for Hypnotherapy and Psycho-Spiritual Trainings
www.hypnotherapytraining.com hch@hypnotherapytraining.com

Reef Karim, MD
The Control Center
www.doctorreef.com www.thecontrolcenter.com reef@doctorreef.com

Harva Kendrick, MA, MFT
www.harvakendrick.com hkendrickmft@gmail.com

Ginny Mosby, MA, MFT
Community Presbyterian Counseling Center
www.cpccounseling.com

Sandra Rasmussen, PhD, RN, LMHC
www.williamsvillewellness.com sandra.rasmussen@waldenu.edu

Kimberly Young, PhD.
Center for Net Addiction and Recovery
www.netaddiction.com

Organizations and Publications

Coalition Against Drug Abuse
www.drugabuse.com

National Institute on Alcohol Abuse and Alcoholism
www.niaaa.nih.gov

International Association of Eating Disorders
Professionals Foundation
www.iaedp.com

National Council on Problem Gambling
www.ncpgambling.org

Society for the Advancement of Sexual Health
www.sash.net

Association for the Treatment of Tobacco Use and Dependence
www.attud.org

The National Association of Addiction Treatment Providers
www.naatp.org

Addiction Treatment Magazine
www.addictiontreatmentmagazine.com

To find a therapist:

American Psychology Association
www.apa.org

American Mental Health Counselors Association
www.amhca.org

American Association of Marriage Family Therapy
www.aamft.org

National Association of Social Workers
www.naswdc.org

Psychology Today
www.psychologytoday.com

ABOUT THE AUTHOR

SHOSHANA KOBRIN, MA, MFT, was born in Johannesburg, South Africa. After taking a master's degree in literature, she pioneered a multi-cultural communications program during apartheid in South Africa. Her manual, *Communicate While You Teach,* was written for teachers and nurses in training. Interest in intercultural group dynamics led her to a master's degree in psychology at John F. Kennedy University, Orinda, California.

Kobrin sees herself as a healer, utilizing the modes of psychotherapy, Reiki, writing, presentations, workshops, and music. She specializes in food addiction, and art and writing therapy. Kobrin is also certified in clinical hypnotherapy and EMDR. She teaches at university level, is an intern supervisor, and provides continuing education for therapists and nurses. A Reiki practitioner, she treats both people and animals.

For 32 years, Kobrin has been teaching, training and speaking to groups, as well as facilitating workshops and retreats professionally and in the community. She's presented at twelve, statewide, professional conferences. *The Satisfied Soul GuideBook: Your Path to Transformation* is a user-friendly journaling book. Two of her books address food addiction: *The*

Satisfied Soul: Transforming Your Food and Weight Worries and *Love, Anger, Power – and Food!* and *A GuideBook for Women. The Satisfied Soul in the Corporate World*, a novel, and collections of poetry and short stories are in progress.

Reading and writing have always been an important part of Kobrin's life. Invaluable tools for healing from an abusive childhood and a long history of bulimia were Natalie Goldberg's *Wild Mind* which introduced her to free, associative journaling; Buddhism's Vipassana meditation technique; Reiki training and practice; and chakra healing.

Kobrin's spiritual and creative life, which she defines as "connection in many spheres of life" is of prime importance to her. She lives in Walnut Creek, California, and enjoys lap swimming, hiking, choral singing, jazz piano improvisation, ceramic sculpture, and watercolor sketching.

On her website (www.shoshanakobrin.net) you can purchase her books, sculptures, ceramic meditation objects, courses, and meditation videos and audios. Read her weekly blog articles and take the opportunity to receive her bimonthly newsletter.

www.ingramcontent.com/pod-product-compliance
Lightning Source LLC
Chambersburg PA
CBHW070350070426
42446CB00050BA/2787